Sports and Your Child

Sports and Your Child

What Every Parent Must Know

J. R. Bishop
and
Cliff Schimmels

OLIVER
NELSON

A Division of Thomas Nelson Publishers
Nashville • Atlanta • Camden • New York

Published in Nashville, Tennessee, by Oliver-Nelson Books, a division of Thomas Nelson, Inc., and distributed in Canada by Lawson Falle, Ltd., Cambridge, Ontario.

Printed in the United States of America.

Library of Congress Cataloging in Publication Data

Bishop, J. R., 1938–
  Sports and your child.

  1. Sports for children. I. Schimmels, Cliff.
II. Title.
GV709.2.B57   1985   796'.01'922   85-13815
ISBN 0-8407-9527-0

To our families,
who loved us enough to tolerate us
through both victories and defeats,
and to our players, coaches, and trainers
—past, present, and future—
who somehow always made us look smarter
than we really are!

Contents

PART FOUR: Sports Opportunities

Introduction

As a high school football coach, I have had several bad nights. But this night was one of the worst. When the game with our arch rivals began, my defensive hopes were on our halfback. An all-conference senior, he was a coach's dream—quick, intelligent, dependable. He was "indestructible." He never got hurt, never even got nicked. But in the middle of the first quarter, he bruised his knee and was out for the rest of the game. I did what I could. I took two Tums antacid tablets and sent in the second-string defensive back.

He was a nice young man, a sensitive sophomore who eventually became a good player. He worked hard in practice. But since he played behind a seemingly invincible senior, he wasn't prepared to take a serious role in a ball game. That night he lived out his fears. And mine. The opposition found him quickly and threw pass after pass toward his corner of the field. Early in the fourth quarter, just as the other team had thrown a third touchdown pass over his head, the young man came loping off the field, head held low. Tears rolled down his cheeks.

Just as he neared the sideline, a cross spectator bellowed her insensitivity, "Who is that kid, anyway?"

One of the assistant coaches, better known for his quick wit than for his tact, yelled back with equal force, "Just some mother's baby boy, lady. Just some mother's baby boy."

Since that night, I have wanted to shout out that truth to fans everywhere, to parents, coaches, recruiters, referees, and often the players. It is the battle cry for this book.

Written for parents whose children are already interested in sports—as well as for parents who would like to spark that interest—*Sports and*

1

Your Child is full of suggestions: how to pick a sport best suited to your child's talent, how to train, how to choose the right places to play, where to go for special training, how to develop special talents, how to buy equipment, how to accept the joys and frustrations of participation, how to put sports in the proper perspective, how to live with an athlete, how to accept coaches, and how to get the greatest emotional and social benefit out of sports participation.

As parents as well as coaches, we recognize that an athlete, whether great or small, All-American star or Little League bench warmer, is still "some mother's baby." We base our suggestions on what we would want for our own children.

Active interest and participation in sports can be valuable to a child's growth, but it can also be oppressive. Too often, fans, coaches, and parents project their own personal expectations, whims, goals, or fantasies onto the young athlete. A child should not be expected to fulfill someone else's dream. That takes the fun out of sports. And fun is the primary reason for sports.

As you guide your son or daughter from childhood through adolescence into adulthood, you will supervise and perhaps engineer some of his or her experiences in sports. Athlete or not, your child must live in a world of sports. Our culture is saturated with sports and sports talk. Americans have a faithful and compelling love affair with athletes and athletics. You may want to protest that it shouldn't be that way, but it is so nevertheless.

Major televised sporting events—like the Super Bowl or the World Series or the Olympics—attract the largest viewing audiences. Newspapers devote entire sections to sports events, analyses, and personal glimpses of star athletes. An interesting comparison is to check the space given to sports coverage against the size of the business section in the local newspapers. Our children choose their heroes from the world of athletics. In the early 1970s, random high school students were polled to determine the current heroes of American young people. The most popular choice was football great O. J. Simpson.

Just recently, I held an informal session with the male members of a church youth group. Some were athletes and some were not. As the conversation turned to models of Christian faith, however, every one of those young Christian boys chose his models, not from ministers or missionaries or biblical heroes, but from professional athletes who profess and practice Christianity. Sports exert a powerful influence on the lives of our children.

Language is filled with sports allusions and references. Our talk is casually decorated with such expressions as *bat a thousand, go for the gold, k.o., kickoff, par for the course, pinch hit, strike out, tackle, team players, throw in the towel, toe the line.* The list goes on, but this is no recent phenomenon. References to sports can be found in the languages of most cultures, particularly those with a written literature. In the New Testament, for example, the Apostle Paul talks about such things as "running a race," "working toward a prize," and "wrestling with principalities."

Sports are as integral to a culture as music, art, and literature. To understand a culture, it is important to know the games played and the emphasis put on those games. (How can one understand the British if one doesn't know the term *sticky wicket?*)

Sports may assume an even greater importance among adolescents. Success in a sport is the quickest, most effective way for a junior-high or high-school student to achieve recognition and social status. Success can provide such a boost to self-concept that the probabilities for achievement in other areas of a young person's life, including academic studies, are enhanced.

Graduate and professional schools, including medical and law schools, look for well-rounded students. Some give special attention to prospective students who participated in sports during their high-school and college careers.

Occasionally, critics claim that sports are over-emphasized in schools. That may be true, and I am sure that it is at times. Often the cultural interest in sports imposes an emphasis on participation. Schools respond to what they feel their communities want. The activity led by the most excited teachers is the activity emphasized in schools. And the communities get excited too. I have taught in schools that committed most of their attention to band or speech or science or, in one rare case, business courses. The reason is clear. The community and the people in charge of those programs were excited about what they were doing, and they excited the students.

If the community or the coaches are excited about sports, sports will get attention. With that kind of attention in the environment, your child is going to have some kind of a relationship with sports. If that relationship is positive, your child can profit as participant or as interested fan. On the other hand, if that relationship is negative, harmful lessons and attitudes can result. We don't want that to happen.

As coaches, we see hundreds of young people a year who use the sports experience as a route to happiness, success, and positive growth. We would like that to happen for your child. That is our motive for writing this book.

Sports and Your Child is divided into four sections—Part One: The Sports Scene; Part Two: Sports and the Family; Part Three: Sports and the Body; and Part Four: Sports Opportunities.

Each section gives specific information and suggestions. Each chapter concludes with answers to questions asked us by parents over the past twenty-five years. This book is general. We want to give you enough information to get you and your child started right.

If you feel that you need more information on a particular topic, check your library or bookstore for more specialized books.

In the meantime, we hope you enjoy being the parent of an athlete. But more importantly, we hope your child has fun in sports. If that is the case, you both will learn some valuable lessons.

PART ONE
The Sports Scene

1. *Joys and Frustrations*

Anything that demands so much attention and occupies so much time as sports has to be good for something. If you have a child who is about to start a life of sports or has already started one or is being urged to start one, now is a good time for you to consider the first and probably only important question you can ask: "What can my child get out of a participation or interest in sports? What good can come from that relationship? What harm can come of it?" But we don't want to answer that question now. Let's just concentrate on the possible positive values of sports to your child.

Fun

We are coaches. We are now college coaches; but we have been junior-high coaches, high-school coaches, park-league coaches, and semi-pro coaches. We make our living by convincing young athletes that they must beat those folks down the road. We work hard at that objective. But in spite of all our hard work, and in spite of all our emphasis on our objective, we still believe that the first and only reason for sports is to provide athletes and fans a good time. Throughout this book, we will give you some suggestions for making your child a better athlete, but our first goal is to give you some suggestions for making your child happier. If happiness isn't a natural by-product of sports participation, then either sports are wrong for your child or the strategy is wrong.

Of course, fun is not to be understood as some momentary, hedonistic, pain-free, glorious, sensual romp. Hard work goes with good times. Sometimes fun exacts a price of sweat, pain, tears, and a few hard struggles. But if the eventual reward is strong enough to withstand the continuing effort, then your child is having a good time.

Even if a million-dollar pro contract looms in the future, your child still deserves a good time. After all, even the pros "play" their games.

Conditioning

Are you surprised by what some young athletes can do? I am. Of course, we "old-timers" like to get together and tell ourselves that in *our* day, we were stronger, bigger, quicker. But we weren't. The records tell us that. Today we know more about the human body than we ever have known before. We know more about conditioning and foods and everything healthy. We have better equipment and better coaching.

If all that knowledge, all those advanced techniques, and a workout schedule, are followed, your child's health and conditioning will definitely improve. Tasks and responsibilities can be better performed with more of this created ability. If your child's tendency is to sit quietly and enjoy huge doses of television, encouraging interest in a sport may be just the thing to make your work as a parent easier. It's possible that a great interest for exercise and physical activity can be developed. Getting in shape is more fun if you know you are going to use that conditioning to achieve success and stardom and attention.

On the other hand, practicing and playing a competitive sport may not be enough. Your child can definitely get into condition by working hard in preparation for the sport. But if there's no conditioning, the sport by itself won't work any magic. A person doesn't get in very good shape standing in right field all night watching fireflies chase each other. Conditioning is a part of sports participation, but it isn't a given. The athlete has to work to stay in good enough condition to be healthy.

Basic Human Values

Every year our college junior varsity football team plays the state prison team. We always have to go there because the team sponsors don't let those guys travel much. The experience is good for our young athletes. Every year when we first arrive and survey the opponents, however, I go through the same agony. When I see the size and speed and age and raw ability of those men on the other team, I get a lump in my throat. I thank God that the mothers of those college kids weren't allowed to come and watch this. Those prison guys are big. And they're good.

But we always win. Every year we beat the bigger team. I asked their coach about that, and he told me the reason. Only two men out of more than two thousand in the prison have ever played high-school football.

Maybe, just maybe, participation in an organized sport does teach a person some valuable lessons about how to adjust and function and live in society. We coaches want to believe that. The players and parents want to believe that. Former players want to believe it.

I would like to tell you that sports participation always teaches such lessons as discipline, integrity, hard work, unselfishness, teamwork. I would like to tell you that sports offer the only classroom left for teaching those lessons in our society, that if you want your child to learn those lessons, you will, if necessary, hogtie and carry your child right now to the nearest ballpark. Some coaches have made that very claim.

But I am not going to tell you that. At least, not that way. First, if I told you, you wouldn't believe it. You read the papers. You read about the escapades of some coaches and pros, those people who have been in sports all their lives. If sports can teach such noble lessons, why didn't these characters learn anything from all their association?

No. I won't tell you that sports *always* teach those lessons, but I will tell you that sports *can* teach those lessons. If your child tries hard and has a good example at home, if you find a good coach who understands people and sports, and if you maintain a parent-child relationship close enough to provide constant feedback, your child can learn such lessons as the rewards of hard work, the value of unselfishness, and the pleasure of persevering. Many athletes do. But when they do, most of the "ifs" I listed are met.

A Sense of Belonging

Everybody has to belong to something. Although those of us who make our living working with young people are particularly conscious of that basic human need, I suspect that adults also like to feel that they have membership and acceptance and identity within a specific group.

Among young people, children and adolescents alike, that need to belong is so powerful that peer acceptance becomes a driving force. In order to belong, some adolescents wear the right clothes; some drink or smoke; some join gangs or clubs; some play sports. Throughout this book, we will talk about the social repercussions of sports identity. In fact, all of Chapter Seven is devoted to that topic because this is a definite factor in your child's decision to play a sport.

How to Live with Competition

This is such a big topic and such an important point that all of Chapter Two is dedicated to it. Here, I will just mention it as one of the lessons and urge you to read the next chapter.

Frustrations

Throughout this book, we will frequently point out the joys and thrills of sports participation. But since we are equal-time writers, we will pause here to remind you that all those great joys can backfire and create some real emotional problems for some children. Remember that when your child enters the sports world, you are each taking a risk. The charm of the sport is very appealing, but it doesn't work well for everyone. Consider the following situations:

- The other day, one of the local high-school football teams lost a game by a score of 88 to 0. Now, put yourself in the moccasins of those parents who had to live with those players that night and the weeks to come. What would you say to them? What kinds of activities would you plan in an attempt to help them regain some sense of self-worth?

- A girl joins her high-school basketball team. Since there aren't too many girls in the program, she makes the squad, but then she spends every minute of every game sitting on the bench. She doesn't get to play in a single game. Try explaining to her that sports participation is a sure route to peer acceptance. As she is sitting on that bench game after game, she is probably experiencing some of the most intense pangs of rejection any human being can feel. For her, this subtle form of rejection is particularly painful because she has attempted to achieve distinction but failed. What would you say to her?

- In the final moments of the final game of the state basketball tournament, the star player makes a bad pass. The opposing girl steals the ball and scores the winning goal just as the final buzzer sounds. In the dressing room afterward, the players at first sit in a stupor of shock. Then they cry. I ask you: Is this fun? Can this be healthy? Is this good training for these young people? Is this preparing them for life? I don't know the answer to any of these questions, but I would like to know what you are going to say to your daughter when she gets home that night.

I remind you again. When your child decides to participate in sports, a chance to learn some great lessons and accumulate a whole storehouse of happy memories goes with that participation. But on the other hand, it may not happen that way. There is always a risk.

Because of the intensity of the sports experience itself, and because of the risk involved, being a parent of an athlete is a special role within the larger role of being a parent. You must assume the additional burden of knowing as much as you can about sports and how they work. But you also need to know how your child works. You need to know how intense the feelings, how deep the anxieties that inevitably will surface through the association with sports.

Sure, sports can help you in your role as a parent by providing you with a good classroom to teach some rather noble lessons and to give your child a spare time activity. But regardless of how good the program is and how good your child is, sports won't raise your child. You still have to assume that office by yourself.

Your job in being the parent of an athlete is to anticipate, suggest, monitor, and encourage your child in the sports experience. You will always want to know how good your athlete is—strengths, weaknesses, response to winning and losing. You will want to know how success is measured and how competition is handled. Since that last issue is so important, it will be the topic of the next chapter.

What Parents Ask

1. *I put my son into a youth baseball program because I want him to learn courage and tenacity. But he never is allowed to play very much, and he says the other players make fun of him. He wants to quit. Should I let him?*

   Immediately! Hear what he is saying to you. He is learning rejection, hostility, and anger. He can get those lessons anywhere, so he doesn't need any more of them from an activity that is supposed to be fun. Let him quit now, and maybe he will try again when he grows a bit.

2. *My daughter loves to play tennis, and she has worked herself up the ranks. But she hates to lose. When she does lose, she cries a lot and is in a bad mood for several days. I don't know whether her tennis success is worth all that pain on her and on us.*

   It is! Look, your daughter is getting the good lessons. She is just overreacting in one small area. If she didn't have tennis, she would still have to deal with this attitude somewhere else. Encourage her to stay in tennis, but help her learn to control that fear of losing. Some professional athletes have written excellent books that could help her.

3. *If I let my son play football, will he be a better man?*

   Who knows what influences a person's growth or attitudes? But I do know that having good parents is more important to a young person's growth than playing football.

4. *My thirteen-year-old son is a sports nut. He isn't very active himself, so he will never be a very good player, but he spends all his time in sports. He reads the papers, collects posters and cards, memorizes the averages. He talks about sports all the time. Is this kind of activity healthy?*

   Sure. It is a lot healthier than some other hobbies he could get into. In fact, some adolescents achieve about as many values from a sports *interest* as they get from *participation*. Think of all the nonplaying career opportunities in sports—writers, coaches, administrators. He may be on his way to success. Don't discourage him. And whatever you do, don't ever throw away his collection of cards. Some of those old baseball cards are more valuable than oil and gas leases.

2. *Competition*

At the base of the Washington Monument, I waited in line for an elevator trip to the top. I wanted to experience that panoramic view of our nation's capital. Since it was a rather busy summer day, the wait took almost an hour. Two young boys in front of me, who appeared to be about seven years old, entertained themselves by playing the old over-and-under hand slap game. They had worked out a rather comprehensive set of rules and a point system, and they kept a running score. The winner won the opportunity to enter the elevator first when our turn came.

As I watched those two children playing as they waited patiently in a rather hot sun, I thought of the pros and cons of competition. In recent years, some people have claimed that competition is harmful to emotional growth. In the mid-1960s this attitude grew so powerful that some state-school activities associations dropped contests for such things as music and speech and began to hold festivals. Instead of naming a first, second, or third place winner in an event, the judges awarded a I, II, III, or IV rating based on the quality of the endeavor. Thus, there were no winners and losers. At least, that was the way the idea was designed to work. Coaches and students, as well as communities and school boards, still added up the number of I's to see who actually "won" the festival.

On the other hand, some people insist that competition is necessary, even exciting. Since our children will someday have to compete for jobs, salaries, promotions, mates, sales, and parking places, we cheat them if we don't provide them with the opportunity to learn how to win and lose, even if it means becoming tough-minded or (even worse) getting boxed around at times.

I am no big fan of either extreme, so let me state my middle position and the thesis of this chapter as simply as I can. We can't deny the role the competitive spirit plays in our lives, but we shouldn't ever allow our-selves to become victims of it. This is what we need to teach our chil-dren, particularly as they discover the world of sports.

Knowing the Opponent

Competition can be divided into three classes, according to who is the opponent: (1) competition against other people; (2) competition against a standard; and (3) competition against oneself and one's own ability.

Although these three classes are not always totally distinct, one is usually more dominant than the other two. In fact, most of us usually think of sports competition in that first class only—where someone beats someone else and where winners and losers are named.

We may tell ourselves and our children that it doesn't matter whether we win or lose, rather it is how we play. But we really don't be-lieve that.

History only records the final score. Actually, we probably recite our little cliché as a rallying cry. We know that if the athletes play well, they win more than they lose.

But even contests at this high level where there are clear cut winners and losers—including such sports as basketball, football, tennis, base-ball, and wrestling—are still filled with subtle moments of competition from the other two classes. Regardless of the score, when the batter smashes a grounder down the line, that third baseman is not thinking in terms of winning and losing. At that moment, he is alone in the world with this opportunity. Nobody can help him. Nobody else can take the blame or the credit. He either makes the play or he doesn't. And that is the thrill of competition against the standard. Regardless of the score, an out is an out. A good play is a good play. The third baseman knows that.

The most successful high school basketball coach I know never talks to his team about winning or losing. He tries never to mention the words. Rather, he posts a list of game objectives before each contest. This list includes such things as offensive rebounds, defensive re-bounds, field goal percentage, free throw percentage, turnovers, and steals. If the players meet the objectives, they have met the standard they were competing against. Of course, they also win the game in the pro-cess.

Some sports, particularly those with definite measurable times or weights or distances, lend themselves more to competition against the standard. For example, I have been known to run a marathon. Of course, at my age and size, I do enjoy beating people, but I actually run against two standards.

First, I want to finish. After that I want to finish in less than four hours. This is the par concept in golf. Since four hours is the accepted par for struggling marathoners, I compete against that standard more intensely than I compete against the other people in the race. In golf, I may be trying hard to defeat a specific opponent, but I am still always conscious of par, that standard commonly used to judge excellence.

These measurable sports also offer a better opportunity for athletes to compete against themselves. Swimmers, runners, weightlifters, jumpers, and the athletes who throw things in track meets are always competing against the toughest of opponents—their personal best. Sure, they like to win the event and hang the ribbon around their neck. But all of them can tell in an instant how close this performance came to the goal they had previously established for themselves.

Some critics give the impression that the only ugly or ignoble competition is of the first class, where we compete to beat someone else. But whether or not we choose to acknowledge it, the other two classes of competition can be just as intense and just as psychologically demanding.

In the 1984 Olympics, one swimmer won his race easily. Think of that. This young man was a gold-medal winner in the greatest sports contest of all, the Olympics. And he will go down in history for his achievement. But at the end of the race, when he learned that he had not set a new world record in the process, his visible disappointment was recorded on television for all to see. The competition against himself gave him a far tougher opponent than any in the pool with him.

Lessons of Competition

This kind of competition against standards or against one's own goals can be a driving force, inspiring your young athlete to push himself toward maximum ability. But it can also be a terrifying, debilitating, psychological master.

As you talk with your child about competition, and you attempt to teach the principles you endorse, you may find it helpful to break the contest down into its individual moments so the young athlete can see each moment as a subtle example of one of the three classes of competition. This also may help your child put the eventual outcome in proper perspective.

1. Competition Teaches Us to Accept Success and Failure

Let's face it. If your child competes in a sport—or anything else, for that matter—winning or losing is inevitable, regardless of the opponent. This is a rule of life. With a combined total of nearly fifty years in the coaching profession, we authors have never had a season in which we didn't lose some and win some.

On the whole, adjusting to the wins has been easier than adjusting to the losses. Nevertheless, most people still need some special training in how to live with success. It isn't so automatic as it sounds. This is particularly true when a team or an athlete is encountering a long string of successes.

In a winning situation, two things can go wrong. Although the pressure of long-term success is never so powerful as the pressure of long-term failure, it can still build to such a pitch that the athlete may begin to dread the next contest, to fear putting past success on the line. This is tough pressure. The second problem with too much success is that the athlete may become complacent—and complacency is the harshest form of arrogance. Success may come so easily that competition loses its challenge. There simply isn't anymore growth. Persons who allow themselves to grow complacent from too much winning are going to meet frustration somewhere, because competitors will eventually catch up.

Adjusting to losses is always a little tougher than accepting success, but this, too, can be learned. The first task is to determine why the losses are occurring. Perhaps a simple mistake is made, or the chosen competition is better than anticipated. In this case, an honest assessment of ability is needed. Perhaps preparation isn't correct. In this case, the athlete has control and ability to change conditions until the right approach is found. Or perhaps a losing attitude has been developed. A losing attitude is not natural or God-given. A losing attitude that won't permit pushing to the point of success has been learned. And if it has been learned, it can be unlearned and replaced by a winning attitude.

Accepting oneself, even after a loss or setback, is a vital part of participation in any sport. An athlete has to learn how to regroup and start all over again with a new zest. And this is a valuable lesson for any child to learn, because failure will be met often in the process of growing.

But the most difficult adjustment may not be to winning or losing, but rather to the *possibility* of winning or losing. For many children and adults alike, the *fear* of failure is more devastating than the *reality* of failure. I worked with a young man in a sports camp. He was rather capable athletically and could have been reasonably successful among the competition at the camp. Unfortunately, however, he was constantly obsessed with the fear of losing. This fear was so strong that he eventually quit trying. He has a problem much bigger than sports, and this problem could haunt him in most of his adolescent activities. I am sure that he is terrified of the grading system in school. How can this poor fellow get up enough courage to risk asking a girl for a date?

During the week of camp, we went right back to competition to help this young man overcome his fear. As often as we could, we took him aside and let him perform in timed trials by himself. He even won some medals performing under those conditions. When the boy and the camp personnel were confident that he could compete and achieve at least some success, we moved him into direct competition with other people. Although he lost a few times, he also won enough times to indicate that he was about to overcome his fear of failure. This is just one example of how sports can help a young person learn to accept success and failure.

2. Competition Provides an Opportunity to Evaluate Abilities

There seems to be a natural human need to know what we are capable of doing and how good we are at doing it. The only way to discover this is to test our many abilities, either against some fixed standard or against someone else. And this is competition. Sports provide the perfect setting for us to learn how to do this. We can use these opportunities to test ourselves physically and athletically; then we can use that same method of testing to assess our other abilities, such as intellectual or artistic.

But the one thing to keep in mind throughout this whole process of testing by competition is that we are only discovering our ability or talent in one specific area. We are not measuring ourselves as human beings or as God's creatures. If we have a specific talent, good. But if we don't happen to have it, we should also be able to accept that fact without deep depression or despondency.

In running marathons I have discovered that I am better than a few, though definitely not worldclass caliber. I could stay awake at night and worry about that, but it wouldn't do me much good. It is a simple fact of life. In the area of long distance running, I know my talent. Through competition, I have acquired an objective evaluation of that ability. I can live with myself.

People trained in sports competition seem to have a definite advantage in this respect. They can take honest evaluation or criticism without translating that criticism into a personal attack.

In our college's education department, seniors go through an extensive and intense student-teaching internship. College professors assigned as supervisors offer evaluation and encouragement to these beginning teachers. Each semester, even the nonathletic professors ask to supervise athletes. The reason they give is always the same. Athletes can accept criticism.

Sports competition can teach us how to evaluate our talents or abilities, yet keep that evaluation separate from the entire picture of who we are as special creatures of God.

Dangers of Competition

Now that I have convinced you that competition is a good teacher for you and your child, let me caution you that competition can also become an unrelenting taskmaster. As your child enters the world of sports, you need to look for the balance. Two common dangers are possible from too much competition or too much emphasis on competition.

1. The Competitive Spirit Can Become an Addiction

I have seen young people who have become so caught up in competing that they simply can't function without it. They depend solely on competition to provide them with a basis for their feelings of self-worth. They have no definition of themselves outside the activities in which they compete. This is very similar to an addiction to gambling. These young athletes thrive on the risk and on the possibility of winning. If they can't make an activity competitive, they can't even participate. And so they make competitive games of everything—school work, leisure activities, even rest.

Several years ago an educator dreamed of a noncompetitive world where young people gathered in the streets or on the lawns or on the beaches and entertained themselves by casually tossing each other flying disks. Well, his dream of flying disks became reality. But notice how often Frisbee games turn into cutthroat competition with elaborate rules and distinct winners and losers.

2. Competition Allowed to Run Rampant Can Become All-Consuming

Athletes can become victims of their own competitive zeal. When this happens, the compulsion to win can cause a person to lose sight of all other values of participation. It is this extreme, "winning is everything" attitude that gives all competition such a black eye. Unfortunately, too often when we speak of competition, people immediately remember the stories of absurd demands, cheating, cutting corners, taking every possible advantage to win.

But the point of this chapter, and the point of this whole book, is that competition doesn't have to be this at all. We are probably all born with a bit of a natural competitive spirit. Very early, babies learn to compete with their siblings for attention, with each other for toys, or with other distractions in order to get their needs met. And we can't change this. Beyond this natural spirit, our attitudes toward competition are learned. We pick them up through the years. If we have the right attitude toward competition, if we know how to handle it, how to use it, and how to learn from it, we have learned this attitude. On the other hand, if our attitude is not very wholesome, we have learned that, too. And that is a promise of hope for you as a parent.

Teaching the Proper Attitude

You can teach your child the proper attitude and approach toward competition. Of course, sports are competitive. The very nature of athletics puts your child in competition against some opponent. But with your help, your child can achieve a healthy knowledge of self-worth in God's universe. Let's conclude this chapter by looking at some specific suggestions for things you can do to teach your child this balanced outlook toward competition.

1. Emphasize the fun of doing. Sport is a process, a game, and if we are playing for the right reasons, we ought to enjoy the process regardless of the outcome. Always help your child see the fun in playing.

2. Play board games or card games with your child. Don't make a big deal out of winning or losing, but don't deny your child's privilege to lose once in awhile. Actually, start this as early as possible with your child.

3. Treat your child the same after wins or losses. Be careful. You may have to work at this, but it is important. Make sure that your love and your gestures of love are not based on how well your child performs. If you usually go out for an ice cream cone after a game, go out even after your Little Leaguer strikes out with the bases loaded, one run down, in the bottom of the last inning. Your love and recognition are especially needed then.

4. Never make gifts and rewards contingent upon winning or losing. There are enough people putting this kind of pressure on your child, and it certainly isn't needed from the parents. If your child deserves a new bicycle, buy it—but don't say you will buy it if the team wins the city conference or some such nonsense. Giving a gift for winning not only overemphasizes the winning, but it also takes the fun out of winning. Winning a game should always be its own reward.

5. Help your child make an honest evaluation of his or her ability. You don't have to be cruel or frank, nor do you need to take the romance out of the unmeasured factor we call desire. You do need to help your child understand that self-acceptance does not depend on abilities. Sometimes we get into a competitive situation where we are outmatched no matter how hard we try, and a good pep talk doesn't do much good. We just need to accept ourselves and live with it. Because of this honest evaluation, your child will be in a better position to deal with personal strengths and weaknesses. Every athlete does parts of some tasks better than others. Strengths can be used to compensate for weaknesses.

6. Make sure your child enjoys some successes along with failures. If your child isn't succeeding at all, it may be that the sport is wrong. If that is the case, you will want to look at Part Four of this book.

7. Make sure your child has an opportunity to watch well-known athletes—college, Olympic, or professional—either alive or on television or on videotape. From watching them, your child will learn that everyone wins and loses, that even the pros strike out with the bases loaded in the bottom of the last inning.

What Parents Ask

1. *My daughter started gymnastics years ago and she is very good. But she refuses to enter a meet. What is wrong with her?*

Maybe you should ask, "What is right with her?" Apparently, she is competing at the best level. She has taken charge of her own body, and she gets her joy out of making it work the way she wants it to. For her, the sport is an art. Isn't that great? I wish all athletes could enjoy their sport at that level.

2. *Are some sports just naturally more competitive than others?*

No! People who play bring the intensity of competitiveness to the sport.

3. *If a person is highly competitive in sports, does that mean that person is competitive in everything?*

In other words, would I do business with someone who cheats in golf? Sports may provide a good indication of a person's spirit of competitiveness, but not always. Some people can keep sports as a separate area of their personality.

4. *Does a person have to be aggressively competitive to succeed in athletics?*

No. I referee basketball. I would much prefer to referee varsity over intramural games because those varsity players are rarely so aggressive or angry or vicious or tense as those intramural players. The more experienced athletes have learned how to handle competition.

3. *The Winning Attitude*

"No, I wasn't surprised when they came from behind to win the championship game in the final quarter. *These kids are winners.*"

"When I recruit a high-school player for my college team, one of the most important statistics is *how many games his team won.*"

"She's not too strong or too quick, but *she doesn't like to lose.*"

"Winning is contagious."

The *winning attitude* is a rather mysterious, unmeasurable factor of success.

I do not know what it is for sure. My win–loss coaching record indicates that I don't know how to manufacture it. But I have been close enough to the winning attitude to know it when I see it. I also have been close enough to the opposite attitude to see the difference quite plainly. Through experience with hundreds of teams and thousands of players, I have learned something about the difference between winning and losing attitudes. I know the power of those attitudes in sports success.

Observations About the Winning Attitude

The following points won't paint a thorough picture of the winning attitude, and I have no sure-fire suggestions for producing one where none exists. I do, however, offer the following observations for your consideration.

1. The Winning Attitude Has Little to Do with Natural Athletic Ability

Among professionals who represent the top one percent of world athletes, some winners have a winning attitude. On the other hand, some winners don't have such an attitude. In the most casual junior high intramural teams in the nation, some players have winning attitudes. Some don't. Although such traits as size, strength, and speed may contribute to the winning attitude, those traits don't necessarily mean that the possessors will be winners.

2. A Fine Line Separates Confidence and False Confidence

Confidence is an absolute must for athletic success. False confidence is the monster of losers. Unfortunately, the two appear so alike that it takes a lot of experience and frustration to distinguish between them. I have been tricked. I have prepared football teams that I thought were ready. All week long in practice, there were little demonstrations of enthusiasm and chatter and big talk. "Boy, we are going to beat those guys." The players' demonstration of bravado convinced me. We were ready. But when we got off the bus, sized up the opposition, and started doing our calisthenics, my players' voices were so high they could have sung soprano in the church choir. We were in for a long night.

False confidence not only seems sincere, but it can get ugly at times. Sometimes false confidence comes across as arrogance. Real confidence rarely does. Unfortunately, the athletes themselves frequently don't know the difference between false and real confidence. Since they know how to get ready for a contest and build their confidence, they go through all the steps. But sometimes the steps don't work, and so they go to the contest with a false hope that flies away at the first sign of adversity.

3. Winners Experience the "I Can Do It" Moment

I run marathons and so have occasions to talk to other runners. Most of them are better than I am—about an hour better than I am. But regardless of how good we are, most marathon runners share a common moment somewhere in the course of every race. It is that moment when in sheer exhaustion and exhilaration we muster enough mental energy to see the climax and say to ourselves in full and real confidence, "I can do it. I can finish."

I watched a tennis match between a relatively unknown high-school player and a ranked college player. At first the college player was winning easily, but the high-school player came on strong late in the match and swept the last set. I asked her the reason for the turnaround. She said, "I suddenly realized I could beat that girl."

As a coach on the sidelines, I have watched this moment a thousand times. It is always exciting when an individual or a team suddenly reaches that realization, "We can do it."

Over the years, I have come to believe that every winner reaches this conclusion. It may be sometime during practice or the contest itself, but every winner has it. The opposite attitude—"We are going to lose"—likely results in just that. I have had teams that have had that attitude even when we were twenty points ahead. Just as predicted by their own attitudes, we lost.

4. Winners Take Advantage of the Moment of Risk

In any contest between two people or two teams, there always occurs that single moment when the action changes, when one of the opponents changes from passive to aggressive play. In a basketball game, for instance, one girl may be dribbling against another in the full court press. If the defensive girl is going to steal the ball and accomplish her mission, she has to take a risk. She has to choose the right moment and become the aggressor. She has to reach in. If she has the skill and is good at timing, she makes the steal. If she isn't good, and the other girl takes advantage of the moment, then the opponent scores an easy basket unguarded.

In a tennis game between two nearly equal opponents, there is that moment when one of the players quits lobbing and smashes the ball. If the hit is good, the aggressor wins. If not, the player is out of position for the return.

In football line play, if the defensive player is going to get to the quarterback and make the sack, he has to make a move. During that move, he leaves himself vulnerable; if he wins that moment, he achieves the glory. If he loses that move, he gets a face mask full of sod.

Winners have an instinctive knowledge of timing and of making the most of that moment of risk.

5. Winners Relax into Intensity

Ever since I have been in this profession, I have heard big-time coaches talk about the intensity factor. It sounded so impressive that I have even begun to talk that way. "Halfway through the third quarter, we lost our intensity." "If we can hold on to our intensity, we will pull this one out." "Don't lose your intensity out there. It is our biggest asset."

I have used the language all right, but until recently, I didn't know what I was talking about. I always thought that since *intense* sounded like *tense*, the words meant the same. But they don't. In fact, those two terms are almost opposites. I learned this difference yelling from the sidelines, "Let's get intense." Well, when I yelled that, my players got tense instead of intense.

I am not trying to be cute here. There is a factor called intensity, and it is a valuable tool in the winner's bag. I have seen it. I have had teams devastated by another team's intensity. I have coached teams that accidentally stumbled on to moments of intensity and went on to victory. I have seen football teams so intense on any given series that no matter what play was called, it worked. I have seen basketball players so intense that they were going to score regardless of what the opposing players did. I have seen tennis players who were so intense that you could look into their faces and see they were going to win the point.

But whatever that emotion of intensity is, it isn't tense. Athletes don't become intense by being tense. They become intense by relaxing into a mental state of determination and confidence. This is the quality that we coaches would like to create or maintain. Unfortunately, I haven't seen a coach yet who knows how to turn intensity off and on at will. But just understanding the difference between *intense* and *tense* has helped me become a better coach, and perhaps that same understanding may help you become a better counselor and comforter to your child, the athlete.

I realize that just listing some observations about the winning attitude doesn't offer a thorough definition of this rather mysterious trait. But this listing should help you understand a little more about what is happening.

Developing a Winning Attitude

Now that we have at least begun to reach a common ground for understanding the term *winning attitude,* the next question is, "Can we do anything about it? Can we help an athlete (or anyone, for that matter) develop a winning attitude?" I am glad you asked that question because I have been asking it myself through the past twenty-five years of my coaching career. Although I have not come up with any foolproof prescriptions, trial and error, observation, and winning and losing have led to my developing a short list of essential activities. These activities contribute to the development of those traits held in common by all winners.

I do want you to realize that this list is a private and personal secret, and I would like for you to honor my request for confidentiality. Please don't show this list to any of the people we play on our regular schedule. I don't want them to learn what I already know about winning. That would just make them tougher to beat.

1. Physical Conditioning

Getting in top physical condition is good medicine for almost anything that ails an athlete. If you don't believe it, try it. When we are in good physical condition, we feel good about ourselves and have more confidence. When we are in a better frame of mind and not quite so defensive, we are more objective about accepting our strengths and weaknesses. These feelings contribute to the winning attitude, whether it's in sports or some other endeavor. But since sports is physical by nature, top physical conditioning is the first requisite to the winning attitude. The athlete has to feel equal to the opponent in strength and endurance. If confidence is missing at this level, it won't just happen to pop up elsewhere in the game. You can assist your child in developing confidence and a winning attitude by helping to maintain a training schedule for achieving top physical condition. (Part Three offers some definite suggestions in this area.)

2. Skill Development

Some athletes have more natural physical prowess than others. They are quicker, more coordinated, stronger, and they have better body control. On the other hand, some athletes have *better skills* than others, but they have learned those skills somewhere. Every coach I know has thousands of stories about athletes with average ability who made themselves winners by learning skills and techniques: The mediocre hitter whose batting average increased one hundred points after learning to bunt; the mediocre basketball player who led the team in rebounds after learning to block out the opponent under the basket; the mediocre sprinter who became a state champion hurdler after learning the hurdle steps. Notice the emphasis on the word *learned*. These skills are learned. Although some people may naturally learn more quickly than others, any person with average ability can develop skills sufficiently to gain an advantage over the more naturally gifted athlete who has not mastered those skills.

So how is a skill learned? That's easy. Get some instruction on the right technique. That shouldn't take long. After that, it is just a matter of practice, practice, practice, practice, and practice.

If you are interested in your child's becoming a winner or developing a winning attitude through athletic participation, one of your major tasks is to make sure that the skills are practiced. I will cover this further in later chapters, but I want to warn you here. If you send your child out to play any youth league sport without having provided an opportunity for practicing the basic skills, you should be arrested for child abuse. I have seen that child, standing out in right field in the middle of a ball game, surrounded by watching playmates and friends, and that poor kid has never seen a fly ball, much less caught one. That is criminal. No one should do that to any human being.

If you don't have time to go out in the backyard and practice with your child, pay somebody to do it. If you can't afford to pay somebody, hold your child out until a little brother or sister gets big enough to be a practice partner. But don't let your child go into athletic combat without having practiced the basic skills first.

I intended to put this parental warning in stronger language, but I toned it down a bit. I hope you get the message anyway.

3. Successes and Challenges

To develop a winning attitude, your child needs to win—against *good competition*, against *a challenge*. If it is just a matter of winning, parents and coaches could probably arrange it. We could line up a schedule that would provide our young athletes with easy victories. But that isn't enough. To develop a winning attitude, the athlete needs the challenge of good competition—competition that requires pushing to the limits of physical and mental ability. Winning too easily will make one arrogant and sloppy. Winning against a challenge will make one courageous.

I once taught in a small community that took pride in its school basketball team. When the new coach came to town, he matched his young team against the biggest, strongest teams that would agree to put us on their schedule. Throughout the season, we lost a few games because we played among the best. But when we went to the state playoffs and started playing schools our size, we not only were a better basketball team, but our players had developed a winning attitude toward the competition. Enroute to the state championship, we beat five previously undefeated teams. We came from behind four times. We won three times in overtime. Our players and our team had a winning attitude.

The winning attitude is a strong force. It is an essential key to success in sports—and an important value to be gained from sports participation.

What Parents Ask

1. *My daughter plays on a soccer team that hasn't won a game all season. Could this damage her self-image?*

   It could, but it probably won't—not if you and her coach handle matters properly. Sometimes, in fact, this kind of experience can build as much character as a winning season. I once coached a basketball team that didn't win a game all season, but those young players were able to keep that in perspective and learn from it. They are now happy, successful adults.

2. *My son has played on winning teams all his life. Does that mean that he will always be a winner in whatever he tries?*

   No! That doesn't even mean that he has a winning attitude. You can, of course, help him learn from that experience, but the experience by itself won't teach him what you want him to learn.

3. *Is a winning attitude inherited?*

   I doubt it. Perhaps living in a house with a certain attitude will help that child form a good attitude toward sports or other matters. But then, it doesn't always happen that way.

PART TWO
Sports and the Family

4. *Parent Motivation*

Before you and your child leap into the sports world up to your necks, you need to back off in a corner somewhere alone and ask yourself an important question. It may be one of the most embarrassing questions you will ever have to ask yourself as a parent: "Why do I want my child to participate in sports?"

Don't cheat. Be honest. You may find your answer a little shocking.

To help you get started on this little task, let me offer you the following test. I have listed eleven reasons why parents want their children to participate. Study these reasons; then rank them from one to eleven based on their importance to you. Again, I urge you to be honest. You are alone. No one will ever know.

____ 1. You want your child to get into shape.

____ 2. Your child asked to participate in this sport and really enjoys it.

____ 3. Your friends recommended it.

____ 4. You want your child to learn the lessons of competition, teamwork, discipline, and good manners.

____ 5. All your child's friends are playing this sport, and you want your child to be accepted in their group.

____ 6. Your child needs to learn how to play alone and with others.

____ 7. You want to be a part of your child's sports participation by coaching or cheering, and this is the sport you know best.

____ 8. Your family needs the central focus of your child's participation.

_____ 9. You want to get your child out of your hair for a while.
_____ 10. You want to be the parent of an all-star athlete.
_____ 11. Your other child was a good athlete.

Okay, I hear those protests. The test is too hard. Ranking is not a fair measure of how you feel. You have several reasons for encouraging your child to participate. I know all that. Yet the test is important. Sure, you may endorse several reasons and reject some. But by establishing a definite list of your own priorities, you can simplify your role as a parent. You need to know where you stand and how you feel _before_ your child (a) doesn't train as hard as possible, (b) loses, (c) wants to quit, (d) sacrifices school work to spend time on sports, (e) misses supper every night of the season, (f) dominates the television choices, (g) gets hurt, (h) gets so upset about not being good enough that crying becomes a bedtime ritual, or (i) gets cut from the team.

If you begin by knowing your honest reasons, you are better prepared to respond to some of these emergency situations. And they _will_ come up.

You also will be in a better position to see if your expectations for organized sports are realistic. You may be expecting too much or too little, and you may end up being disappointed with the whole endeavor.

Why Do You Want Your Child to Participate?

Although some of these reasons will be covered more fully in later chapters, let's examine each item individually to establish its reasonableness and possibility.

1. Fitness

You want your child to get into shape. This idea does have possibilities in the world of sports. Playing baseball or swimming or swinging on the bars develops some strength and stamina. But just playing the games or going to the meets and spending the rest of the time sitting in front of the TV isn't going to be enough activity to do much good. If participation in the sport isn't motivation to practice and work out, the sport simply won't satisfy your child's need for physical conditioning.

2. Enjoyment

Your child asked to participate and really enjoys the sport. This is probably the only "right" reason on this entire list. If your child makes an independent decision to participate in a sport and tries hard, you can expect physical, emotional, and intellectual growth to result.

But now, you have another small job. You need to help your child think through the decision to participate. If the reasons are not all that valid, interest may wax and wane with every moon change. For example, if your child really likes the sport, perseverance will be far more likely than if participation is based on social reasons or is endowed with some false idea of glamor and future fame. Disillusionment can set in fast.

3. Friends' Recommendation

Your friends recommend it. Let's face it. This is one of the worst reasons why parents force their children into sports. In fact, it can be downright cruel. So little Johnny down the street is having a wonderful time playing summer baseball. Big deal. So his mother is always telling you how happy her son is and what a wonderful time he is having and how easy he is to get along with since he has discovered himself in his sport. I have good advice for you. Stay away from that woman.

You know your son or daughter better than anyone else in the world. Use the knowledge and understanding that grow out of your love to help your child establish goals and dreams. So you forfeit one topic to brag about at the office or at the daily neighborhood coffee break. Is it better to forfeit a conversational topic than to forfeit your child's happiness by forcing unwilling—and unreasoned—participation.

4. Worthwhile Lessons

You want your child to learn the lessons of competition, teamwork, discipline, and good manners. First, I commend you. These are worthwhile lessons, and people do learn such things from sports—particularly if these lessons are allowed to be the result of, and not the rationale for, participation. These lessons can be learned in other ways. Your child has a good chance of growing into a responsible human being even without sports. These lessons are not automatic results of sports participation. They are taught—by you. You have to teach your child teamwork, whether through sports or other activities.

5. Peer Acceptance

All your child's friends are playing this sport, and you want your child to be accepted in their group. I used to think peer pressure was a curse of adolescence, but I have changed my mind. I am not an adolescent anymore, and I still spend a lot of my time and energy trying to win friends and influence people. In this effort, I even find myself doing things I really don't enjoy doing very much. About once a year, I go out and spend the better part of one whole day playing golf. I hate golf. I am not very good at it, and I fail to see the point. But I go because I want to be buddies with the people who ask me to go with them.

Your child is not all that different. Playing sports is a direct route to social acceptance. In fact, that is such an important issue, all of Chapter Seven is devoted to it.

6. Play Skills

Your child needs to learn how to play alone and with others. Actually, I like this reason, particularly if it is valid. But first you have to decide who has the problem—your child or you. Is it a question of not knowing how to play or of not knowing what you want? The distinction needs to be clear.

Frankly, we Americans have some serious problems with childhood. We are not much in favor of letting children be children, and we often become impatient with childish play. Because of this, we are not very observant or understanding about what children do to entertain themselves.

For example, watch pre-readers play cards or board games. They somehow know there are rules; but since they don't know them, they just make them up as they go along. "See, I have a two and that means you give me three cards." Or "You have a one and that means you win the game." They are happy playing with their own rules. If some well-meaning adult taught them the real rules, these children probably wouldn't enjoy the game any more than before. In fact, if you left them alone, they would probably go back to their own game.

I have seen several youth baseball parks where no Frisbee throwing is allowed. That is obviously an adult rule. Since some of those little Mickey Mantles would rather be throwing a Frisbee than playing baseball, that Frisbee could be a disruptive influence on their play. In other words, they would be playing child's play instead of adult's play.

So before you force your child into organized activities, make sure you are using the right definition of *play*. There is no real reason to disrupt a child's self-made enjoyment just to teach some adult games.

7. Your Own Expertise

You want to be a part of your child's sports participation by coaching or cheering, and this is the sport you know best. I would guess that even if this was the real reason, you didn't put it first. Most parents don't have enough courage to be that honest. But if you do have such feelings, you need to lay them out so you can deal with them.

Actually, the solution is rather simple. You really don't need to burden your child with your own ambitions in the sports world. If you want to coach, volunteer. Someone can use you. If your child wants to play, fine. If he doesn't, that won't hurt your coaching or cheering career. But it is simply not fair to force a ten-year-old into some activity so you can live out your own fantasies.

8. Family Focus

Your family needs the central focus of your child's participation. This issue is too important to cover in one small paragraph, so all of the next chapter will deal with the impact of sports participation on family life.

9. Baby Sitting

You want to get your child out of your hair for awhile. Don't believe it. Organized sports is not a baby-sitting service. If you are not willing to make some personal sacrifices, your child will not get very much out of the sport or be very happy in it.

Again, this will be described more fully in the next chapter, but your child's decision to participate in any organized sport will affect the entire family structure.

10. Fame

You want to be the parent of an all-star athlete. When I first realized that my son wasn't going to be an all-American, I became angry at him. He just wasn't trying hard enough. Eventually I worked through my frustrations. I am not angry anymore. In fact, I like my son, even if he didn't set any records. After all, I am young yet. I can wait for my grandchildren.

I make this little confession only partially in jest. I really did have those feelings. I suspect most parents do. But such feelings must be controlled. Growing up is tough enough without the added burden of having to carry one's parents' fantasies around. Those dreams of stardom could build a wall between you and your child and ruin your whole relationship. You don't need that, and your child doesn't deserve it. Whether your child is great or can't play a lick, develop your relationship, your love, and your friendship on some other basis than sports alone.

I could tell many sad stories about what has happened to people who have tried to achieve fame or popularity through their children's athletic ventures. We all know those stories. But if we don't guard our own feelings carefully, we could fall into the same trap.

11. It Runs in the Family

Your other child was a good athlete. This is the cruelest reason yet. In fact, it may even be blasphemous. God didn't create any two people alike, and asking a child to copy the gifts and abilities of a brother or sister is a burden no one should have to carry.

I give this warning as harshly as I can because, unfortunately, parents can fall into this trap so easily. Especially if you are a sports nut, you will always find it easier to be pleased with the achievements of the athlete in the family than with those of the nonathlete. And you will probably show that favoritism.

If you have a child who happens to have gifts other than athletics, force yourself to learn to appreciate those gifts. Enjoy that child as affectionately as you love and like the athlete. This is a strong warning from a parent, a coach, and a friend of children.

As you go back and look at the way you ranked those eleven items, you may want to ask yourself one final question: "Is my interest in my child's participation for my benefit or for the child's?" If you answer that question correctly, you must now do what you can to make sure your child gets the most out of the opportunity. To do that, you need to consider what you and the rest of the family can do to encourage and support the endeavor.

What Parents Ask

1. *How early can I start buying my three-year-old child gifts like balls and sports equipment in order to build an interest?*

Buy him anything you want to, but don't put any great expectations on those gifts. They may help your child develop an interest and live out your fantasies for you. But they may not. Are you prepared for that?

2. *I finally persuaded my junior-high daughter to try basketball. She is now out for the team, but she won't try very hard. I think she is just doing that to spite me. What do you think?*

I congratulate her. That seems to be a fairly common way for a young person to get rid of the burden of an overzealous parent—to fail and then the parent will stop pushing. But I do have a suggestion for you. If you enjoy basketball that much, you play. Don't base your love for your daughter on something as insignificant as what she wants to do in her spare time.

3. *I'll admit I want my son to play soccer, but I have kept quiet about it. I haven't said a thing. Why does he still accuse me of pressuring him?*

You probably are. In a thousand subtle ways! What we parents think we do is one thing. What children perceive is another. Children are always telling me about parental demands and pressures. When I ask the parents, they are shocked. If you really want your son to play soccer, I would suspect he knows that. I hope you have a close enough relationship that the two of you can sit down and discuss it.

5. *Family Demands and Rewards*

I called the mothers to tell them that the game had gone into extra innings and their sons would be late for the evening meal. One lady chuckled, thanked me for my politeness, and explained that her four sons were all athletes. For the past eleven years, dinner at her house had ranged from 4 P.M. to midnight. It was rare when two people sat down to eat together. But that didn't bother her, not anymore. She had learned how to cook to accommodate that hectic schedule. It was just something she had to do. She didn't mind. Those sports activities were worth the sacrifice.

I know those four sons. I know what they do and what kind of people they have become as adults. I don't know whether that sacrifice was what made the difference, but fifteen years later something has paid off. They are good and successful men.

This story illustrates a critical point. Your child's decision to participate in organized sports must be a family decision because it has direct bearing on all members of the family. Everybody has to get into the act in one capacity or another.

Time Schedules

The most obvious example of that family decision is in scheduling. Athletes have to practice, play games, and take part in pep rallies and victory celebrations, all according to a very specific time schedule. They can't wait around until the lawn is mowed or dinner is over or the car is free. They just have to be there, and all members of the family must understand this time demand.

I have seen some good athletes drop out of sports simply because the family could not adjust to the demanding schedule. Fathers wanted their children home for chores. Mothers wanted their children home for meals. Or the whole family wanted to take a trip to Disneyland during the week of baseball playoffs.

Before these conflicts arise, the whole family needs to decide how committed it is to that sports participation. Know what you are getting into at the beginning because you can't change your mind in the middle of the season. It isn't fair for you to take your athlete on a family vacation when the team is expecting help in winning a big game. If you don't take your child's commitment to teamwork, discipline, and sacrifice seriously, you can't expect your child to learn those lessons from involvement on the team.

Money Demands

Unless you find some very unusual circumstances, no organized program is without some financial cost. Your young athlete is going to have at least some expense. Of course, you don't have to give in to all the demands. He may need socks, but he doesn't necessarily need the most expensive designer socks on the shelf. She may need a new racquet, but she may not need the one that costs one hundred dollars.

In fact, buying the necessary sports equipment may provide you with a good opportunity to teach your children some important lessons about money. With such items as shoes, protective pads, and helmets, you want to make sure you get the best. You can shop around for prices, but don't cheat on the quality. Other items such as socks and practice uniforms may help you to teach your child to be thrifty. You don't need to buy the name brand if the other will serve the purpose just as well.

If one of your children has a special interest or ability in one of the expensive sports such as gymnastics, swimming, or golf, you have a new kind of family challenge. If the child continues in active participation, you will have to make a financial commitment to it. But then you will have the problem of the demands that are placed on the rest of the family. Regardless of the cost, you may need to convince your family of the value of the expense.

I know a family with a child who has possible Olympic talent in gymnastics. That family is prepared to pay as much as one-fifth of its income on that child. But the parents have also convinced the other children that this is a family project.

Let me also remind you of the always prevalent expense of insurance. Before your child participates in any kind of organized sport, make sure your insurance covers the possibility of injury. If your present family policy excludes that sport, you will want to invest in another policy just for your athlete. This is a must. I am not trying to exaggerate the dangers of sports, but active children get hurt more than those sitting home watching TV. Make sure you are covered.

Training Demands

If you have a child who is participating in sports, some special training procedures will be necessary, and the whole family will have to help. For one thing, athletes of any age need to watch their diets. Young athletes in training also need a lot of sleep. The family will need to recognize and perhaps even enforce early bedtimes. In the sports with strenuous practices, athletes are frequently exhausted after a workout, and this can make a difference in what a family does in the evening. The athletes usually need some quiet and rest after practice.

Practice Demands

Regardless of the sport, no athlete gets enough practice during practice time. If your child plays a sport, at least some of the time at home must be spent practicing. It is most often the personal attention a young athlete receives at home, which team practice opportunities simply don't provide, that leads to improvement in the sport.

I spend part of each summer watching youth baseball. I am always appalled to see those young boys or girls, who have never even played catch, trot out to play a baseball game. There is no excuse for this. If a father or mother is too lazy or too busy to play catch with a child at home, the youth program will serve no purpose except to embarrass or make the child hate baseball. The coach simply does not have the practice time to play catch with every player. That is the job for someone in the family.

If someone in your family can't make the commitment to help your child practice athletic skills at home, then you are cheating that child, not only of athletic achievement, but also of the values sports participation has to offer.

Emotional Demands

My wife and I recently made our first visit to Niagara Falls. We are usually rather chatty people, but as we stopped to view that magnificent spectacle of power we stood in awed silence for almost an hour. This was a moment when the emotions demanded silence. If one of us had broken that silence, we would actually have infringed on the other's right to the appropriate emotion.

Like looking at Niagara Falls for the first time, sports are emotional experiences for the fans, for the coaches, and especially for the athletes themselves. In fact, a sports performance is often as much emotional as it is physical. If your child participates in any kind of organized sports competition, there will be some unusual emotional moments related to that activity. During those times, your child will need special understanding and maybe even some special help from the family.

Different people respond differently to different situations, so it would be impossible for me to make a list of all the emotions your young athlete will experience in such times as before games, after victories, after losses, or before and after practices. But since you as a parent are the one person closest to him, you will probably have a better understanding of your child during those emotional times than anyone else. Thus, you are in the best position to help your child prepare emotionally for competition. You can also help to build an understanding as to why such emotions occur.

In the sports life, there are several very emotional moments. We know about the agony of defeat and the ecstasy of victory. Television has made sure that we all know what the athlete is going through during those special moments. We have all seen the winners go wild with joy and the losers cry or hang their heads in quiet. But television also brings a couple of problems to the reality of your child's sports world. For one thing, the television cameras focus on the winners and losers who make the best show, on those who react most visibly. Television never shows us those athletes who respond to wins and losses without any visible emotional displays. By focusing on the extremes, television could actually be teaching your child to imitate only the emotional responses shown on the screen, and not to express the real feelings that come from within. The other problem with televised reaction is that it never shows the other emotional moments an athlete goes through before reaching the point of winning or losing.

Regardless of the sport, practices themselves require emotional preparation and reaction. Some athletes really have to "psych themselves up" to get through a practice. At the same time, however, practices are always primarily learning situations, and too much emotion can destroy the calm mind the athlete needs in order to learn. A young athlete's family can be of real service in helping to develop the right emotional balance to push hard during practice but at the same time stay cool enough to make the practice session a valuable learning experience.

Another emotional time for some athletes is that special time following a practice. Many go through some of the same kinds of emotions they go through during an actual game. This could be a good time to have a small discussion about the practice. You don't have to make a big production out of the moment, but just take some time to give your child the opportunity to discuss the practice with you. Make it known that you are interested in how your child feels about what happened.

Let's be honest. Some of us don't always have as good a relationship with our children as we would like to have. We are often looking for some common point on which to build a better relationship. The moments following practice times could serve as that starting point for the two of you. Your child may need some special understanding right at that point, and you may find you enjoy being available.

Despite all the television coverage of the emotions at the outcome, the most critical and perhaps most emotional time during sports competition is just before the game. All players prepare themselves in their own unique way, but all experience some emotional preparation.

A dressing room prior to a ball game is a fascinating psychological laboratory. Some players try to stay loose and calm by engaging in small talk. Some excite themselves by listening to music or watching game films or pounding. Once in a while, a very sensitive athlete will simply go off by himself with his own emotions and vomit. But regardless of how they prepare themselves emotionally, all athletes do need to use that time before a game or a match to concentrate. They need to think about what they are doing. Many athletes mentally picture themselves actually completing each move and each situation successfully.

Since the athlete needs a special environment while he goes through this rather intense period of concentration, this puts some demands on the whole family. Everyone needs to understand the pressures of pre-game preparation. So if your young star is hard to live with on game days, you can at least understand the reason. You may want to allow your child more time just to be alone.

Regardless of how that athlete at your house reacts to the various sports situations, you can be sure that at least some unusual emotions are being experienced. Since you and the whole family are an integral part of that athlete's environment, you do have some special demands on you to recognize what your child is going through and to help him or her to understand and cope with what is happening.

Rewards

Sports participation is a family affair. If one member of the family plays, it affects the whole family. Everybody has to get into the act. But just as this participation puts all these demands on the family, it can also have a positive side.

Through the years, I have seen families thrive on one child's sports participation. The family commits itself as a unit to support and encourage the athlete, who then represents the whole family on the field. That child's participation might become the central focus, or at least one of the common issues of the family, so that all members can share in the preparation, performance, and even the rewards. Thus, the family is welded together and becomes a unit through one child in sports. They may all make concessions; eat at odd times; give up Friday nights to go to games together; watch TV together; listen to the athlete's plights and pains; but through it all they become a family.

Of course, this won't be an automatic result if your son happens to decide to play a little summer baseball or your daughter joins the swim team. But if your family needs that kind of shot in the arm, you could use that participation to draw the family together. But you have to be prepared to go to the games, talk about the practices, support, encourage, and share the victories and losses. You just might find the positive family relationships that develop are worth all the sacrifices.

Of course, the athlete has to keep his sports participation in proper perspective, too. This leads us to the next chapter.

What Parents Ask

1. *Last year, as an eighth grader, my son won the junior-high conference mile run. All summer, he has looked forward to high-school track. But now the coaches want him to practice three hours a day. He will never get his chores done. What should I do?*

That is a tough decision every parent of an athlete has to make. You may have to talk with your son and weigh the advantages and disadvantages of his performing. But if you decide the family can't make the sacrifice for him to run track, make sure you have something else to fill the hole you just created in his life.

2. *I have several children. How do I keep the good athletes from feeling superior to those who aren't that good?*

Every person I have ever met has special talent in some area. As a parent, you need to make sure all your children know what their talents are, and you need to be sure you treat all talents equally. If you go to the ball game to watch the athletes, then you also have to go to the library to help the bookworm check out books.

3. *Why is high-school hockey practice at 6:00 A.M.?*

Because that is when the rink is available at a price the team can afford. Is his playing worth your effort? I don't know. One year, I ran a 6:00 A.M. basketball practice for the junior-high players who had been cut off the varsity squad. Some parents grumbled. I didn't blame them. But three of those players were varsity starters in high school. One made all-state. I wonder what those parents thought about their sacrifice then?

6. *Sports and Priorities*

Let me tell you a story. The state high-school track meet and the state high-school music festival were both scheduled for the first weekend in May on opposite sides of the state. On the last weekend in April, the school's best athlete went to the regional track meet and qualified for three events in the state meet. But she was also the lead voice in the school's concert chorus, which would be participating in the music festival.

The coach and the music director spent all week fighting each other and ended up not on speaking terms. They finally agreed to let the student decide for herself, but privately each one called the student and tried to make her feel guilty enough to choose his discipline. The principal was called in to referee, but he didn't enjoy stepping into a buzz saw. He called the parents. They couldn't reach a decision, or at least they didn't agree with each other. In the meantime, the poor student was still singing lead in the chorus and practicing long jumping for two hours every evening, waiting for someone to make a decision for her. Oh, the pressures of being talented!

Let me assure you that this isn't an isolated case. This very scene has happened in thousands of places, and it will happen again. But it teaches us a lesson. When your child adds the burden of sports to an already busy schedule, another lesson will have to be learned, that of establishing priorities and living within the boundaries of a time schedule. Very few people, children or adults, have enough free time to add another ten hours a week to their schedules without making some adjustments somewhere.

Since there are basically two issues at hand, establishing priorities and budgeting time, we will look at each one separately.

Establishing Priorities

I recently took a friend to the ice cream store. Although she is just four years old, she still had to pick one flavor out of the thirty-one available. She had to make a decision. Very early in life we have to learn how to deal with the pressure of making choices. What is most important? What is least important?

You do your child a favor when you teach him how to establish priorities and learn to live with the consequences of decisions. You are actually helping your child achieve a certain kind of personal freedom.

Learning to fit that sports schedule into all the other activities is a good way to learn this kind of lesson. The first thing your young athlete has to understand is that being involved in sports doesn't mean giving up one's place in or responsibility to the human race. Space still has to be made for family obligations, studies, friends, church, and even such things as dating. This isn't always easy. Each influence makes demands and causes conflicts in one's schedule, and no one person can serve them all equally well. As I said earlier, I know situations where high-school students had to drop out of sports because of family chores. But on the other hand, I know people who dropped out of church activities because of the demands of high-school sports.

Of course, the biggest challenge, particularly for the young athlete, is that sports can engulf one mentally. These activities can steal all of a person's mental energy and time so that there is no room for thinking about other things. A sport can simply take charge of a child's mind unless he or she learns how to place the sport properly in a list of priorities.

Sometime in the process of growing into adulthood, your child is going to have to learn how to establish all of those demands into some order of importance. You can help with that. Let me suggest some specific activities.

1. Show Your Child How to Set Goals

This doesn't have to be elaborate or profound or so rigid that it strips the child of any opportunity for spontaneity. But you can help the child look down the road once in awhile. Ask a simple question. "What do you want to do in junior high or high school? What kind of student do you see yourself then?" "If you were an adult right now, where would you want to live and what would you want to be doing?" "If you could do anything you really wanted to do, what would you do next year?"

As the child begins to formulate answers to those general questions, you may want to move into some more specific and realistic goals: "Let's see. With your ability, you really should be able to carry a B average in junior high." "You can run a mile in six minutes this year, so you could probably be able to cut that down to 5:30 by next year."

By establishing these kinds of goals, the young athlete will at least have some idea of what is expected, and so won't have to wander around looking for direction.

2. Teach Your Child How to Make Decisions

Again, this is a lesson that can be learned early and developed more fully as the child matures. Although there are several formulas for decision making, most are similar in that they are based on common sense. We will work with a common model. Help your child to make a list of all her alternatives of action. Help her then list the advantages and disadvantages of each decision. After that, she can pick the one which is best for her and she can work from there. Of course, decision making is a habit formed over several years of practice, so don't expect miracles from a one-shot lesson. But at least you have shown her the model and given her the opportunity to use it.

By teaching your child this kind of decision-making process, you are helping her learn to take charge of her own life. This is important in learning how to sort through all the possible activities, including sports opportunities. Too often younger athletes can get carried away by such things as the appeal of a coach or a program, and then they forget to consider their own interests and abilities. Any deliberate decision-making process should help your child see the choices a little more clearly.

3. Help Your Child Keep Personal Goals

Once your child has made some decisions and established his own goals by putting all his activities in proper perspective, he may need some help from you to keep those goals. For example, if he sets some goals for grades, make sure he keeps them. If the grades fall below his own expectations, then he is probably letting things get out of balance. In this case, you may need to design a special reminder to help him keep the emphasis in proper order.

4. Help Your Child Learn to Evaluate Abilities and Opportunities Objectively

Frankly, some people are playing one sport when they should be playing another. Some people are spending hours practicing a sport when they should be spending that time practicing the piano.

Let me clarify this. I don't think we should ever exclude anyone from playing organized sports in some form, regardless of that person's ability. Sports can teach several lessons that are valuable to anybody. But a child should not be encouraged to practice long hours at the expense of everything else when all that effort isn't going to go anywhere. This is a bad use of time and ability.

Objective evaluation gets tougher the more children you have in sports, particularly if you have at least one gifted athlete. If you are not careful, you could base some parental favoritism on one child's athletic ability and you could put some serious pressure on your other child who is struggling to be mediocre.

5. Insist That Your Athlete Recognize Family Rights

Your athlete may be a superstar, but that should not entitle her to special privileges or considerations. Of course, as I said in the previous chapter, the whole family has to make some adjustment to having an athlete in the house, but that athlete still has to recognize her responsibility to the family.

Athletes shouldn't be excused from chores, family outings, or courtesy and consideration for the rest of the family. If your young athlete forgets to tell you about a special practice, that is his problem. There is no need for you to drop everything just to bend to his schedule. If you refuse to take him, he might learn that he can't control you with his sports participation and he will probably remember to communicate more promptly next time.

Time Budgets

Now that your young athlete has listed all of his activities and responsibilities and has put those in some kind of order of importance, it may be that there is still time to do most of them in spite of the hours given to sports. It is usually a matter of taking charge of your time schedule; let's call it making a time budget.

Among the athletes at our college, some are so busy with their sports that they don't have time to go to classes regularly. Some can make it to classes most of the time, but don't have enough time left to study. Yet others go to class, study, make good grades, date and marry, serve in other organizations, and still distinguish themselves as athletes.

I realize that some people may be more naturally gifted than others, but their biggest "gift," which separates them, is the trait of personal discipline. These people have simply learned to manage their time. And if one college athlete can learn that, all of them can if they want to. It is never too early to teach your athlete the important lesson of budgeting time. Once this lesson is learned, there will usually be enough time to take care of obligations and to participate in other enjoyable activities.

This is actually a rather simple procedure. Sit down with your child and divide the day into chunks of time such as half-hours or hours. Then help to schedule the various activities into slots. Some of these activities such as school and practice will be scheduled daily. Others such as church and scouts will be on a weekly basis. Include family activities such as chores and meals. If your athlete has a favorite TV program, put that into the schedule. And above all make sure you allow enough time for play.

Now that this schedule is made, you will want to teach your child how to look at the schedule as a guide rather than a dictator. Of course, there is always room for flexibility and unexpected events, but this time schedule, held in proper perspective, will help your child develop a dependable routine. And psychologists tell us that almost everyone performs better when working in some kind of a routine. So you will not only help your child manage time so that there is time for everything, you may even end up with a better athlete.

Let's conclude this chapter with a positive illustration. A few years ago a young man came to our college as a basketball player. In our place, basketball is one of the most time-demanding sports because the season is long. The players must constantly be preparing for the next contest. Players have to miss class to travel to midweek games, or they stay up late at night. This young man was a four-year starter and captain for two years. By his sophomore year he was named all-conference. These are not bad accomplishments for any athlete. But in the meantime, he also made good enough grades and learned enough chemistry and biology to get into medical school; he was involved in one of the campus service organizations; he was active in a local church; and he fell in love and married another one of our students.

This young man is exceptional; I won't argue with that. But part of that specialness was learned. He learned how to live with his sports participation and improve himself as an athlete but still put athletics into proper perspective so that he could include other activities in his schedule.

This story sounds dramatic, but it isn't all that unusual. Thousands of athletes manage to succeed in a variety of activities every year. Actually, a tough sports schedule may even help a young person become more rounded and more active simply because in all his busyness, he learns how to set priorities and manage his time wisely. If your child is going to participate in organized sports, this is both a necessity and a goal.

What Parents Ask

1. *Should students have to maintain a certain grade average in order to be eligible for sports?*

Some should and some shouldn't! Just as some people are good athletes and some aren't, some people are good at academics and some aren't. If a good learner's grades drop because of sports, that student's priorities are wrong and need to be rearranged. But another student might be working hard and simply can't master the material. I am not sure we know what we accomplish by denying that student the privilege of doing the one thing he does well. If some student really loves English literature, we don't make him play average football before we let him go to English class.

2. *If I help my daughter set her goals, including sports goals, won't I be forcing my decision on her?*

Good question. I said earlier that parents shouldn't pressure their children into performance. I do see a difference, though, between pressuring your child and helping her honestly evaluate herself and set some goals.

3. *My son has all the indications of being a great football player. With all the scholarships and possible pro contracts, are grades and classes all that important?*

Sure. If he is that good, he will win the Heisman Trophy. Then in all those interviews, someone is going to ask what he thinks of his parents. You will want him to be literate enough to say nice things about you! But seriously, we have all been created with certain abilities. If we cheat one of those abilities to concentrate fully on another one, we have made a mockery of creation. Great athletes can also be scholars, musicians, artists, entertainers, family people, and poets. You may have a great athlete for a son, but you also have a complete person. Don't ever forget that because, if he is great, his coaches and fans may forget it.

7. *Sports and Your Child's Social Activities*

Your child's decision to participate in organized sports will also affect the social aspect of your child's life. Sports friendships are powerful and frequently permanent. In season and out, athletes move in groups. Students at various levels of competition often establish and maintain lifelong friendships with the people on the same teams. There is something about sharing the pain, the glory, and the heartache that binds people together.

As you and your child consider the possibility of sports participation, you need to be aware of two very possible social results from that activity. First, your child's closest friends will probably be fellow team or sport members, and second, your child will assume a different social role among the larger crowd. Let's look at each of those individually.

Sports Friendships

Your child will probably establish friendship patterns from among sports associates. Obviously, this is not a hard and fast rule, but it is a very good possibility. Although it may be more likely in team sports, those athletes in individual sports also have a tendency to grow very close together in the course of competition.

There are several reasons for these developing friendships. One is the simple matter of proximity and association. If your child participates in a sport, a large block of time will be spent with the other people in that sport. Your child will get to know them in ways he can't know other friends, such as those in his school. He will practice with them, play games with them, sit on the bench beside them, travel to and from games with them, and maybe even travel in the same car pool to practices.

But one of the advantages of this is that if you attend the sports events or drive in the car pool, you will get to know those people, too. You will have some idea of who your child's friends are. This is just one of the added advantages of having a child in organized sports. Since we parents know the power of peer pressure, I think most of us would like to have some control over our children's friendship selection. Encouraging your child to participate in a sport will at least give you some control over the pool from which your child will select friends.

Another reason for these close friendships between athletes is the common bond of the sport itself. If your child is participating in a sport, there is a good chance that a lot of mental time will be spent thinking about that sport, or, in the quiet moments, remembering the last practice or anticipating the next practice or game. Thinking about that sport is naturally linked to thinking about fellow participants. But at the same time, those people are thinking about your child, too. With this kind of mental energy invested, friendships can grow quickly and deeply.

There are other common interests that become forces of unity. Reacting to the same coach, working toward the same objective, and sharing goals, victories, and losses are unifying experiences. In fact, two good lessons can come from this mutual sharing. First, the young athlete gets the idea that he is not alone in his feelings or commitment, but at the same time, he also realizes that he can't do everything by himself. He needs help, and to get that help he needs to share himself. People who recognize this will naturally develop close relationships.

But another reason for the development of close friendships in sports stems from an even deeper personal realization. For most of us, sports are activities that will eventually expose us as we really are. Somewhere in the course of the competition, our true personalities will show. We drop the masks, and we become ourselves with all our strengths and weaknesses hanging out for everyone to see.

I don't know about you, but I want a dependable and loving friend around when I cry after a victory or cry after a loss or lose my temper with an official or make a game-costing mistake or vomit before a game or lie in the middle of the floor with a painful injury. Those are personal times that I am not willing to share with just anybody. I want my friends around when I expose myself and my weaknesses, so I am going to be sure to cultivate my friends from the group that is going to be present anyway, my fellow athletes.

All these reasons make sports friendships close and lasting. Now that I have seen that 240-pound giant cry, he and I will always know something about each other that no one else knows. And that piece of information will always keep our friendship deep.

I assure you that your child's participation in sports will have a large impact on friendship selection and response. You need to be aware of this as the two of you consider the advantages and disadvantages of entering the sports world.

Social Identification

Through sports, your child will achieve social identification. Sports participation influences where a young person fits into a social group and how that person relates to peers. During elementary school usually there is not a big social distinction between athletes and nonathletes, but the gap starts in junior-high and increases throughout adolescence. Most high-school and junior-high student bodies are divided into tightly constructed social castes, and it is tough for a student to move from one caste to another at a specific school.

In fact, most student bodies are broadly divided into two classes, the athletes (and their boosters) and the nonathletes. In most schools, the athletes are known as *jocks*. About fifteen years ago, when the term first came into use, it usually conjured up images of big, dumb guys who had nothing much going for them except their bodies. In more recent years, the connotation has changed so that now the term usually designates those people who make significant contributions to the extracurricular activities of the schools. Jocks are the popular class. In most schools, to be a jock is to be a leader. But jocks are also usually expected to be successful in their classes and at least moderately popular with the teachers and administration.

What this means to a junior-high or high-school student is that athletes often form the school leadership and since they have the common bond of sports to unite them, they usually form a rather close-knit group. In other words, the athletes may form themselves into cliques. At least, they are often accused of doing this. Thus, if your child participates in sports, particularly in the junior-high or high-school program, it will probably mean a better chance to gain at least some peer acceptance and maybe even recognition among the other students. This kind of social identification is particularly valuable to new students in school. Changing schools can be socially devastating to adolescents. But athletes almost always make this transition more easily than nonathletes.

One fall a high-school junior from California moved into our small midwestern school. During the first three weeks of the semester, he was a lonely and disoriented young man. Back in California he had been a diver; but since we didn't have a swimming program, he couldn't even gain recognition in sports. Although he had never played football, I persuaded him to take his chances with the only sport available.

He was a fast learner, but by the evening of the first game, he still didn't know enough to play. Despite his inexperience, I decided to let him run back kick-offs. I silently hoped they didn't kick it to him. But despite my hope, they kicked the opening kick to him. In one of the finest displays of open-field running I have ever seen, he ran ninety-five yards for a touchdown. By the end of the game, he was the most popular student in school, and I never noticed his being lonely again.

The interesting thing about these sports friendships and social distinction is that they really aren't based on ability. Of course, the players recognize and respect the gifted athlete even if they don't like the person. But other than that, the other athletes usually achieve their distinction simply by association with the sport.

If all this sounds good to you and you think you would like your child to become part of the jock class and choose friends from fellow athletes, let me throw in one minor problem. Association with a given sport also carries some stereotyping in the minds of both the athlete's peers and superiors. Frequently high-school students will describe another student with a simple reference to a sport. "He's a football player. She's a swimmer. He's a wrestler." And the person at the other end of the conversation nods in agreement as if that is a thorough description of looks and personality. But whether this extra baggage is part of your child's experience in sports or not, acquaintances and probably friendships will certainly develop from that sports pool.

Of course, part of an athlete's social success does depend on how well the sports role is performed, too. Let's take a look at that possibility in the next chapter!

What Parents Ask

1. *All my daughter wants to do is play basketball, but I would like her to do more ladylike things. What do I do?*

   Love her. She is in a healthy activity, and there isn't anything unladylike in basketball. Sports aren't just for boys. At our college, female athletes are some of the most popular on campus. Why don't you get interested in basketball yourself? You may even discover its appeal to her.

2. *My son wants to play football. But I have terrible memories of football players as big, dumb, rude hulks. If he plays, will he associate with those kinds of people?*

   If the football players on his team are big, dumb, rude hulks, he will. Those people will become his friends. In fact, don't be surprised to find out that he already admires them. They may be why he wants to play in the first place. But don't let your prejudice run wild before you find out. Invite some football players over to visit. You may find them to be nice people.

3. *My daughter wants to be a cheerleader. Will this affect her social group?*

   Most definitely! In fact, this cheerleading group may be the closest group in school!

4. *My fifth grade son is the only boy in his class who doesn't play park-district football. Will that make any difference on his friendships in the class?*

   Yes. It could make a big difference, particularly if several of those boys are on the same team. If you want your son to be friends with those boys, and I can see why you would want him to, you may have to work on it. Invite some over to the house and see if your son and those boys can establish a friendship on some basis other than football.

8. *Special Cases: Superstars and Bench Jockeys*

The parents came to my office to talk about their two sons. Now that the boys had reached junior high, each had become something of a problem, but in a different way. The older boy had recently discovered competitive gymnastics, and he was quite good at it. He had natural ability, and he adjusted to the teaching quickly.

At first, the parents were excited. They enrolled him in a good clinic, and they spent many weekends taking this young athlete to various meets where he had performed well enough to distinguish himself and become rated as one of the finest gymnasts in the state at his age level.

Unfortunately, the young athlete began to respond to all that attention as if he really believed he was important. He began to make unusual demands on the family. He lost contact with his own brother. He dropped his old friends at school and made new ones. He insisted on a new wardrobe. He lost interest in his studies and his grades dropped. In short, he was rapidly becoming an obnoxious little brat.

The boy's brother had different problems. In junior high, he suddenly realized that he had no athletic ability. All the other junior-high students recognized it, too. He tried out for the basketball team, but he was the first player cut from the squad. Despite his protests that he was really trying, his physical education grades dropped to a C, and he wanted to drop P.E. If he wasn't allowed to do that, he threatened to quit school entirely. He too had become sullen and moody and difficult to live with.

These two extremes were magnified because the two brothers were so close in age, but the problem is common enough. Most of the comments in this book have been directed toward athletes who perform

55

somewhere in the average range. Now I want to call special attention to those two extremes—those who achieve enough fame and distinction that they fall into the star category and those who can't seem to make the grade regardless of how hard they try.

The Superstar

With all the emphasis on youth sports these days, it is easy for a young athlete to attract a lot of attention. Uniforms, fields, and equipment are first class. Coaches take themselves and their responsibilities seriously. Fans are intense. Newspapers cover the games with pictures and stories. Local champions travel to distant and exotic places to play in playoff games. In many of these scenes, the talented young athletes become heroes, not so much with their peers as with the adults who come out in droves to support them. And in the midst of all this attention, we have a nine-year-old boy or girl trying to figure out what childhood is all about. No wonder the child becomes confused.

Regardless of how old we are or how well trained we are, fame is always hard to take. Many young professionals have almost ruined their careers because they couldn't handle the attention they suddenly attracted. How can we ever expect a nine-year-old to manage?

Let's not kid ourselves. Nine-year-olds are nine-year-olds. Regardless of how talented a young swimmer may be, regardless of how far he has traveled, regardless of all the championships he has won, regardless of all the people who adore him, regardless of how often he has adjusted to the pressures of competition, that nine-year-old still looks at the world through nine-year-old eyes and emotions. We can't deceive ourselves just because some child or adolescent has excelled in some area.

I have seen twelve-year-old students who are brilliant in the classroom, but they are still twelve years old emotionally. I have seen twelve-year-old athletes compete with the poise and grace of a veteran of many years, but they are still twelve years old emotionally.

I repeat this so often here, because we must not forget it. In recent years, well-intentioned parents, coaches, and fans have put entirely too much pressure on talented children by convincing them that they are superstars. This is an injustice both to the children and to their parents.

Several possible dangers arise out of the attention a child receives as a "superstar." For one thing, it can confuse the child. It may lead to feelings of importance that get shot down when the child tries to act important. Second, if we make a child a hero, there are no other thrills to live for. Consider for a moment the talented Romanian gymnast who achieved her greatest glory when she was less than fourteen years of age. After one has once been so famous, what is left for an encore? Such attention can also produce early burnout. Who wants to be an average player again after having once tasted fame?

In fifteen years of high-school teaching and coaching, I have seen this sad story repeated dozens of times. The young athlete starred in high school and drew a lot of attention and praise. Everybody knew him and came out to cheer him. And we all looked forward to following his career because he had worlds of promise. But after a semester or a year of undistinguished college effort, the young hero comes home, to the place where he was once famous, and he begins to live out his life in the shadows of the fields where he used to be a star. Just to keep himself on edge and to keep the memory alive, he plays pick-up games and summer league while the town now raves about its new high-school hero.

Yes. There is a danger in letting a person become a superstar before he is emotionally capable of handling it.

If your child is particularly gifted, develops early physically, or happens to be in a situation where there is a possibility of achieving a lot of attention, you will need to give some special help. Being aware of the possible dangers of this extra attention will probably give you some pointers on how to help the child learn to handle it, but if you need further suggestions, let me offer some reminders of points made in earlier sections of the book. (1) Emphasize the fun aspect of sports. Never let your athlete lose sight of the fact that this is a game and not a life or death matter. (2) Make your child's fame a family project. Get all the family out to the games. Let all members participate in the scrapbook. (3) Treat this child the same as you treat all other members of the family. Don't make any special considerations for athletic fame other than those your child's participation requires. (4) Demand that this child live a balanced existence. Emphasize other activities such as studies and church.

The Bench Jockey

Now let's look at the other side of the problem. Some youngsters simply can't make the grade. Any attempt at athletics presents a real test of their self-concepts and ability to persevere. Brutal evaluation or open rejection shows itself in several forms. The young player-to-be gets cut from the team in preseason. In the pick-up or P.E. semi-organized games, this child is always the last one chosen. Once on the team, most of the child's time is spent sitting on the bench. In some youth programs, the rules require that everyone must play at least a minimum part of the game itself. This should be a bright spot for this special athlete, but instead it is often the most embarrassing time of the game because the better players laugh or criticize or show impatience because the child's incompetence may mess up their chance to win.

Since our culture places such an emphasis on sports, and we hear so many stories about the successes of the good athletes, this kind of treatment can really be damaging to any child's self-concept. Since sports performance is a quick and sure method of achieving self-identity, particularly for young adolescents, these poor people who try and don't make it can have some serious doubts about themselves in all areas of endeavor.

If you see this kind of thing happening to your child, you don't necessarily need to panic; but you do need to be there to help in the crises. (Notice that word is plural. There will be more than one crisis. In fact, there will probably be a different one every day.)

These following suggestions aren't miracle cures for everything that bothers your child, but at least you can make some effort to let him know you understand what is happening.

1. Reasons for Not Succeeding

First, find out why your child isn't making the grade as an athlete. There could be several reasons, some of which might even be corrected.

a. Maybe he just hasn't developed as quickly as his peers. If this is the case, he will probably catch up in a year or two and compete well. In the meantime, you do have to keep him interested enough that he will keep trying until he does grow.

b. Maybe she hasn't developed some of the basic skills of the game. In this case, she needs practice. That can be corrected. Either you can take charge of this or you can get somebody else to help, but you do need to provide your child an opportunity to develop her skills sufficiently to feel good about her play. Sometimes, this is just a matter of an hour or so of individual attention.

Some friends once called me about their son who was sitting on the bench during park-district basketball. I stopped by to see the boy and shoot some baskets. Although he was strong enough to shoot the ball and quick enough to play defense, his dribbling was atrocious. He had never learned the knack of the right wrist action. In about thirty minutes of casual instruction, he picked it up. He was a starter before the season ended.

c. Maybe he doesn't have enough confidence in himself. This, too, is a common problem. Good athletes are aggressive. If a person doesn't have any self-confidence, he simply isn't going to be aggressive enough to win the attention or the confidence of the coach. The therapy for this is usually practice. If you and the child can practice, he might get the idea that he can play.

d. Maybe she is in the wrong sport for her body shape and skills. In this case, you need to do some discreet counseling. You probably can't come right out and bluntly suggest a change in operation, but you might make some suggestions. You might even take this child to a game or match of a sport you think is better suited to her physical ability and personality.

e. Maybe he is never going to be an athlete. I hesitate to say that because I am not sure anyone is qualified to make that judgment until a child is about old enough to marry and raise children of his own. People do change through various stages of development. But if you decide that your child really won't ever be very good, read the rest of this list.

2. Valuing the Team

Help your child see the values of just being a part of the team. The lessons sports can teach our children aren't reserved for the superstars or first stringers. Those lessons are for everybody fortunate enough to be a part of practice and preparation. Even if your child can't be a regular, there is still value in staying with one's commitment. With your help, your child can learn such things as self-control, discipline, the satisfaction of accomplishment.

3. The Value of Team Unity

Help your child see the value of team unity. I know this sounds like so much coach's talk, but a successful team needs all its players, both the regulars and the substitutes. Frequently a team's preparation depends on the intensity of the practice provided by the substitutes. A football coach recently told me of his plight. Although he has a good starting group, his substitutes are too inexperienced to provide his starters with scrimmages.

Anyone associated with the team can make a contribution to its success. I have seen substitutes with such good attitudes that they helped establish a positive tone for a whole team. Convince your bench sitter that everyone on the team is responsible for the wins and losses.

4. Successes of the Moment

Help your child break the contest into moments and celebrate whatever success comes in those moments. Although only a few moments may have been played, you can still pick out something your child did well. Show your child how to make that one moment stand out as a positive experience to remember. In one high-school game, my son played only one defensive play the whole night. The opposing quarterback was going to throw a pass to that area, but when he saw my son just standing there in the way, he turned and threw incomplete to the other side. That night we broke out the chocolate chip cookies and celebrated that great success when my son single-handedly stopped their whole offensive attack. I know it doesn't sound like much now, but it was a good memory for a bench warmer. My son now has a whole collection of those isolated memories from a few moments of play and a lot of riding the bench in high-school football.

5. Achievements in Other Areas

Make sure your child has some way to achieve a self-concept and social acceptability other than through sports. Being a second-string football player isn't so bad if your child is also the best trumpet blower in school. Those things balance themselves out. Everybody has a special talent of some kind. If your child doesn't happen to have the gift of athletics, keep exploring until you find that special area of expertise. Everybody needs to succeed and feel good about something.

I realize that this chapter seems to be filled with simple formulas for rather complex problems. Handling either one of these extremes isn't always as easy as I might make it sound. But the principles are valid even if the results may be somewhere in the future rather than in the immediate present. You must recognize the problem, do what you can, and pray for results.

With the brothers in that opening illustration, the solution was actually rather easy. I called the talented gymnast into my office and complimented him for his success. I encouraged him to try even harder to make himself the best he was capable of being. Then I explained to him that everyone around him had noticed he had let success go to his head.

He said that he had even detected it himself and that he would try to do better. He apologized to me, to his parents, and to his brother, and he started a sincere effort to reestablish himself with his friends.

Although the other boy legally could not be excused from P.E. class, he was urged to join the debate team. Through that participation, he regained his confidence and actually became more aggressive in sports. He never became a great athlete, but later in the year, he was captain of one of the intramural basketball teams. At least he didn't give up on sports altogether, nor did he give up on himself just because he wasn't athletically talented. Through his debate work, he found a source of friends and a way to achieve a special identity.

Since living with and helping a child who fits into one of these extreme categories is a big challenge for parents, the next chapter will be devoted to the special problems of having a child who is a superstar.

What Parents Ask

1. *Is it worth my daughter's effort to keep going out for basketball year after year, although she never gets to play?*

   Only if she enjoys it. Sports have a lot to offer. Sometimes the struggler gets as much or more out of the sport as the star. If your daughter enjoys basketball and is keeping a good attitude, treat her performance as if she is an all-American.

2. *Why does my son insist on staying out for football when it is obvious that he will never be very good?*

   Because it is fun—because he likes being with the guys—because he enjoys football—because he knows it bugs you. I don't know why he insists, but isn't it great that his interest stays high?

3. *My son is a starter on his youth baseball team. On the same team, there is another little boy who isn't very good. The other boys, including my son, tease him unmercifully. What should I do?*

   Thanks for being conscious of the problem. First, put yourself in the place of the parents of that boy. As I said earlier, sports rejection can be the cruelest kind of rejection. Now, talk to your son. Don't expect miracles. Teasing that boy is one way to get peer acceptance. But make sure your son knows how that boy feels. In the meantime, show your son how to be positive. When that other boy does get to play, pick out one small isolated thing he does, and compliment him on that. If you don't overdo and are sincere, your son might get the idea.

4. *My twelve-year-old son has absolutely no interest in sports. Will this make a difference during his adolescence?*

   Sure! But it doesn't have to be devastating. He is probably going to experience all the joys and frustrations of growing anyway. You will need to help him discover what his interests are, and you will need to make sure he knows those interests are important. You will have to work at that because it may be hard for him to find friends who will help him remember.

9. *How Soon a Star*

The day after my son was born, I went to school and invited all the coaches to have lunch with me. We stopped by the hospital on the way to lunch and took a look at my new posterity. I realized it was still too early to know for sure, but I just wanted to see if one of those experts might notice some little something that would indicate future greatness for this one.

I make this confession because I want you to know at the beginning of this chapter that I understand those people who stare at me during my advice sessions as if to say, "But you don't understand. This one is going to be a superstar." Well, if that is what you want and what your child also wants, I hope you get it. Unfortunately, children are rarely as talented in any area as their parents think they are. Once in awhile, a superstar does come along, and the parents and that superstar both need special attention. In this chapter, we will look at how you can tell if you have a superstar and what you can do about it.

How Can You Tell?

Athletic stardom is a combination of three things: natural talent, hard work, and commitment. Let me repeat that. If your child is going to make it big in the world of sports, he or she has to have some natural, God-given ability to start with, has to work hard to perfect that ability, and has to make a commitment to being good.

1. Natural Talent

Since natural talent is the only one of these traits over which we have no control and the one most difficult to define, I will start here. How I wish we had something like a thermometer to measure natural talent! A person could just stick it in the kid's mouth and know the result in a matter of seconds. That would really solve a lot of problems.

But measuring ability is never as easy as we would like. As a coach, I can tell you that assessing the natural ability of any child is tough under the best of circumstances, but objectively assessing your own child's natural ability is virtually impossible.

Let's try to define natural athletic ability. First, it has something to do with size. But when the child is still young, size is difficult to predict. You can make some predictions based on heritage, but physical growth often comes in spurts; and you just never know when the child is going to spurt. Thus, it is not very wise to base your plans on size alone.

If you are really interested in predicting the growth patterns and eventual size of your child, you may want to take a look at some of the studies that try to make predictions as scientific as possible. Usually those studies base prediction on height, weight, and age progression, and such an evaluation may give you a better guess, but timing growth is still only a guess.

Another aspect of natural talent that might be more reliable is coordination. If the child moves with something of a fluid movement from the very beginning, that might be an indication of athletic potential. Look for signs such as early crawling, walking, running, and mastering the tricycle and bicycle.

But even coordination is a chancy talent. Sometimes the uncoordinated child can learn better coordination. Frequently as the child grows into later childhood and early adolescence, height and weight become factors of coordination.

Another characteristic of natural talent (and this one may shock you) is that quality we call sports sense. Through the years of coaching, we have discovered that some young athletes just naturally think in sports terms. In the heat of competition, they make the right decisions and take the necessary steps to win. You may want to argue that this is learned—that the person who has sports sense learned it—but we are not convinced. Most of our college players have been in the game about the same number of years. Yet, some of them are quicker to adjust to our style of play and to emerging situations during the contest. They seem to have a natural sports sense. This is in no way connected with good sense or intelligence. Other players may be brighter in classwork, but these special players have a natural talent for understanding the game and their role in the game. Unfortunately, we know of no way to assess sports sense until the athlete actually begins to participate.

Other factors that researchers have considered in determining natural athletic ability include (1) the ability to start and stop quickly, (2) lateral movement, (3) the ability to run backward, (4) early development of hand and eye coordination, and (5) the ability to jump. In fact, research in this area seems to indicate that experts can predict the speed of an athlete based on his results in the vertical and standing broad jump.

Of course, any one of these skills by itself probably doesn't mean much, but this list should at least help you to learn what to look for as your child develops. From the results of your observations, you may get some idea of how much effort and hard work you and your child should invest in sports participation.

2. Hard Work

Let me tell you a story about natural talent. A friend's son really did have natural talent, but he was producing at zero level in preseason practice. His efforts were lazy, and his interest seemed minimal. I called him into my office to talk with him. I asked him why I had noticed these things about his play. After some discussion, the boy finally said, "All my life people have told me I have so much natural talent that I have come to believe I don't need to practice hard."

Everyone needs to practice hard and show interest and enthusiasm when participating in a sport. With these attributes, it is possible for a child without great natural talent to perform well in sports. I have seen more players who succeed by mental study, hard work, and determination than I have seen succeed by natural talent alone.

3. Commitment

I have already talked about sports demands on family and individual relationships. Here I will refer to them just to say that the superstar has made sports a first priority. The superstar's sport is the biggest, most important activity in life, important enough to sacrifice almost everything else to meet the demands of the sport.

Sometimes, those sports demands are very heavy. Sometimes, they are unbearable. Both athlete and parents must be willing to make the commitment.

What Do You Do If You Have a Possible Superstar?

If you feel that your child has the natural ability and the commitment to do the hard work it takes to develop into a superathlete in some sport, you are just beginning what can be a wonderful, exciting, promising, and potentially frustrating and depressing journey of several years. All children need special attention and special love for one reason or another. But the child with unusual sports ability needs special understanding, encouragement, support, and even supervision. Having a child of special ability is a big challenge for a parent. But some guiding principles might be worth remembering.

1. Use Common Sense

In the beginning, you don't know whether your child is simply above average or whether the talent shown is really exceptional. You will need to approach the whole business with some caution and common sense. You want to provide every opportunity for developing that skill to the maximum. If you are capable of doing some of the teaching yourself, you will want to spend as many hours working in the backyard as both of you can tolerate. But wouldn't you do this with any of your children, whether or not they are extraordinarily talented?

Years ago, a great baseball player explained how he developed skill as a switch hitter. His father and grandfather pitched baseballs to him by the hour while he switched sides. I tried that with my son, and he still can't hit like Mickey Mantle. But it doesn't matter. We enjoyed the time together.

Keep your child in the mainstream of life as much as possible. Don't have two sets of rules, one for the athlete and one for the rest of your children. Help the young, successful athlete learn to look beyond success to define self-worth on some deeper and more stable factor than athletic glory. For most athletes, that period of intense glory is brief in the terms of a complete life. Make sure your child has a means for happiness after the athletic career is over.

2. Get the Right Kind of Instructional Help

Coaching is better today than it has ever been. We have more knowledge about how the body works. We have extensive research on training and conditioning. Cameras and television tapes provide athletes and coaches with an opportunity to study form and competition.

If your child shows a large measure of natural ability or strong interest in a sport, take advantage of the best possible coaching. Superstardom is partly a factor of natural ability, but every athlete has to master a whole range of skills on the road to success. Often the difference between great and merely good is a skill or flaw that could be corrected with good coaching.

Shop for a coach just as you shop for a doctor or a new car. Ask local coaches and athletes. Go to your library and look for magazines that cover that sport only. If you can't find what you are looking for in the magazine itself, call the publishing company and ask to speak to experts in residence. Since most sports now have a national office designated for the purpose of promoting the sport and offering advice, you can call that office and talk to experts. The people who love the sport don't want to lose any potentially good athlete. If your child has the potential of being good, the sports officials want to know about it.

Many young athletes today leave home to enroll in schools and clinics where they receive high-level instruction for special skills. Several of the United States gymnasts in the 1984 Summer Olympics had been enrolled in these schools. Their success indicated the results of proper coaching and training. Young tennis players have been doing this same thing in recent years. I think we will see more and more of this in the future.

Another area of special instruction is the one-, two-, or three-week summer camp that stresses specialization. The number of these camps held every year is increasing. Since I will discuss these in a later chapter, I will only mention them here.

3. Always Provide the Child an Alternative Life

Regardless of how good any athlete becomes, stardom is at best fleeting and full of potential dangers and heartbreaks. If you do not take care to encourage and nurture other interests in your child's life, you are both in for some misery.

You may notice that I put the burden on parents to provide this alternative outlet. If your child is particularly gifted in athletics, that gift will attract the attention of a lot of people—coaches, press, fans—but you are the only one who will truly understand that "he is just some mother's baby boy." If you lose sight of your child as a sensitive, warm, feeling human being and see only a physical machine, no one else will remember, either. Even sensitive coaches have professional jobs to do and other athletes to coach. And fans are always fickle.

I once attended a track meet to watch a great miler perform. This young man had thrilled fans across the world. During this particular race, he pulled a muscle and had to drop out. The fans booed. What did they know about the agony and the humiliation of some mother's son?

Let me conclude on a positive note. Kenny's father had been an all-American football player and a starter on the NFL Champion Cleveland Browns. Kenny had visions of following in his father's footsteps. I remember the first time I talked with his father about Kenny's potential. His father was then coaching a football team in the Midwest League, which was a minor league to the NFL. He was going to be gone a lot of the time. He told me that I would have a great deal of influence on his son. However, he never made me feel inferior to him as a coach. I told him that I wanted to make Kenny a quarterback instead of the fullback that he had been. Kenny's father trusted my judgment.

It is very important to the coach to know that the parents have confidence in him. So I started my grooming of Kenny as a quarterback. He became an all-stater and accepted a scholarship to a major university. Then things changed. Kenny injured his knee in his sophomore year and never regained his old form. His opportunity for making the NFL—a lifelong dream—was not going to be.

But Kenny had learned to cope with adversity. He had been taught that there was more to life than athletics. He knew his family loved and supported him no matter what he did on the field. He had chosen a university that would meet his needs in areas other than football. He continued to enjoy his college experience and graduated. Even though he did not have great success at the college level, he maintained a positive mental attitude and thus had a happy experience. This is what sports should do for our young people; their athletic experiences should help them to adjust to their lifetime goals, regardless of whether they are stars or just lucky to get in the game when the score gets out of hand.

What Parents Ask

1. *Are stars born?*

   Yes and no. Being a star is a combination of a lot of factors all coming together through something of a mysterious process. To make real stardom, an athlete has to have a ton of natural talent. But then, it also takes a lot of hard work and the right attitude.

2. *My four-year-old is quicker and stronger than any four-year-old child I have seen. Does that mean he has star potential?*

   Possibly, but not necessarily. If he continues those patterns and develops the right attitude toward sports, he just might make it. But children grow in spurts. Don't build too many hopes until you see how he grows.

3. *Since my four-year-old is advanced for his age, is it necessary for me to get him into sports as early as possible?*

   No. My approach is simple. Sports, particularly for children, should be fun. Thus, I think the child should develop his own interest. There are far more dangers in starting a child too early than in starting one too late. Don't get caught in some of those dangers. Use your child's interest as a deciding factor on when to start.

PART THREE
Sports and the Body

10. *Conditioning*

"If we can keep it close, we'll win in the fourth quarter because we are in *better condition* than any of our opponents."

"We have so many injuries this season. We must be doing something wrong in *our conditioning program.*"

"I want all of you to report on the first day in *top condition.*"

"When the runners get to the three-quarter mark, *condition* becomes a factor."

"It is so hot today. The *best-conditioned* team will win."

"I am sorry I can't come to church this morning. I raked my leaves yesterday and I am sore all over. I am just *not in as good a condition as I was* in my playing days."

What is this mysterious but powerful tool called condition? How does one get it and how does one lose it? For the purposes of this book, I will define *condition* as the ability of the body to respond to the physical demands made on it. That includes muscles, tendons, and joints, but it also includes the heart, lungs, and even the mind.

Every day as we learn more about the body, we learn more about the nature and process of conditioning. Consequently, principles for conditioning change often. But the results are obvious. Presently, athletes are accomplishing feats never thought possible until recent years. Our young athletes are stronger, quicker, and faster and have more endurance than ever before.

Of course, this knowledge produces a whole litter of conditioning theories. In fact, there are about as many conditioning theories and programs as there are athletes. One of the toughest tasks facing an athlete or the person who helps the athlete train is to sort through all those different theories and programs and pick out the best one. But in the end, no conditioning program is worth much unless the athlete applies himself to it.

About three years ago we bought a stationary bike for our house, thinking that everybody in the family would jump on the bike and get in great shape. But it hasn't happened that way. Not one single member of the family is in any better condition than when we bought the bike. Of course, altogether we ride it about three miles a year. Conditioning takes commitment.

Regardless of all the scientific talk and all the promises, any sound conditioning program begins with two objectives. First, it will develop the athlete's body to the point of a good ability to perform well in that athlete's sport and help to minimize the risk of injuries. Second, a good conditioning program will help the athlete, particularly the young athlete, develop a sense and an appreciation for a conditioned body, not only for sports participation now but also for the years afterward. I am serious here. It doesn't do us much good to get a sixteen-year-old into basketball or figure skating condition only to have that athlete become fat and sloppy and die of a heart attack at the age of forty.

I urge you to keep this perspective in mind. Your young athlete is a precious human being who has a whole life to live after active sports are over. You must keep that perspective because coaches and that loud-mouthed fan at the football game and even your child can't look at it that way. Those people can only see the present. Since they can't see the future, you must.

Any conditioning program depends on the person and the physical demands that must be faced. Many preadolescent children get enough physical exercise just being children. They run and skip and yell enough to keep their muscles and lungs in fine tone.

But the more inactive ones may not get enough exercise to keep themselves physically sharp enough to meet the rigorous demands of a youth sport competition. These children will need some kind of formal conditioning program. Without it, they won't be able to perform as well, they run a greater risk of injury, and they won't have the confidence needed to enjoy competition.

If your child seems to be in good enough shape to enjoy whatever activities are pursued, then you don't have to worry about formal conditioning. If not, you may want to start a conditioning program even before your child reaches adolescence.

Now, to help you with your decisions, let's talk about some specific conditioning projects.

Strength Training

To make a muscle strong, you have to work it. A muscle that has been trained, worked, or developed is both stronger and more dependable than an untrained muscle. An untrained muscle may work effectively once or twice, but it will tire quickly. So the athlete with the trained muscles will be able to perform effectively for longer periods of time. The most common way to train a muscle is through some form of weight training.

As in most areas of conditioning programs, weight-training theories, equipment, and programs abound. You and your child can only pick one. Most of them are sound and effective if the athlete believes in the program and obeys the warning signs. To help you sort through some of these, let me make some observations.

Principles and Values

1. A muscle grows strong as it works against resistance. Thus, weight training is asking a muscle to do more work than it is used to.

2. If a muscle is asked to work near the maximum of its potential, it will get bulky. Thus, athletes who want bulky muscles (football players, for example) lift heavy weights. Athletes who want strong, flexible muscles work with less weight but use more repetition.

3. To understand any of the different weight theories, you do need to understand a few basic terms. The *max* is the maximum amount of weight a lifter can lift in any given exercise. How the max is determined and how often depend on the particular theory the athlete is using. *Reps* (or repetitions) are the individual times a lifter lifts a certain weight in succession. A *set* is that number of times. In other words, three sets of ten reps means that the athlete lifts the weight ten times in succession, rests, and repeats that two times.

Every theory of weight training uses its own particular approach to the prescribed amount of weight, sets, and reps. If you want to understand this in detail, buy one of the many books available that cover this area, or go to the high-school coach and ask him to explain his theory.

4. Since a strong muscle is more easily controlled, the trained athlete should actually be quicker as well as stronger.

Equipment

1. *Universal Machines.* About twenty years ago, some people took several different weight-training exercises and built them into one single machine called the Universal Machine. This process made weight lifting convenient and safer for those teams and private clubs who could afford one of the machines. The Universal Machine has a minimum of five training stations, so five athletes can be working at the same time. Those stations include bench press, military press, leg press, curl machine, and inverted sit-up board. Since the weights are built into the machine, they can't fall off and smash someone's foot. Since the weights are easily adjusted, athletes of various strengths can be working at the same time. Since five athletes are working around one machine, they can encourage one another during the process.

Despite all these advantages, the Universal Machine doesn't seem to be as popular to some athletes as it was a few years ago. The sophisticated weight lifters and muscle developers tell me that there is a psychological thrill in seeing iron being hoisted. Since the machine can't provide that thrill, some lifters prefer something else.

2. *Nautilus.* The Nautilus equipment presents another form of weight machines that are much more sophisticated. There are about as many different Nautilus machines as there are muscles in the body, so if you go to a Nautilus center, you can work the muscle you are actually going to be using in your sport. In fact, you can even make it work the way you will need it to work in actual play. For example, a tennis player can find a Nautilus machine that will provide resistance for the exact movement of a tennis swing.

3. *Free weights.* This is sophisticated sports talk for bars with removable weights on each end. For serious weight lifters, iron is everything. (That is why they call it pumping iron.) For the weekender or novice, sand-filled weights can be bought, which are less dependable but a whole lot cheaper. Sand-filled weights do tend to shift their weight and lose weight, so if you think you and your child will be serious weight lifters, a good set of iron weights may be worth the initial investment.

To make the best use of free weights, one needs at least a bar and as much weight as the athlete can lift. One also needs a curling bar, a couple of hand bars, a squat rack, and a bench rack. If you don't know what those terms mean, stop by your local high school and ask the coach to take you through the weight room. If it is a wealthy high school, the coach may show you some very fancy manufactured racks. If the high school doesn't have a large sports budget, you may see some interesting creations put together by the custodial staff or shop class. Either kind serves the purpose.

4. *Homemade weights.* If you and your athlete want to do weight training and don't want to spend a large amount of money, use your imagination. Anything you have lying around that is heavy enough to do some good and can be lifted can serve as weight. When I was growing up on the farm, we used hay bales and sacks of seed rather effectively. Of course, we didn't know we were developing strong muscles. We also developed our forearm muscles, so important in baseball, by milking a few cows. See how easy it is?

At my house now, my son and I get quite a lot of mileage out of a pipe with two-gallon buckets of concrete at each end. Considering that we had all the material around the house, our weight set cost about twenty-four cents. A few years ago, two Olympic wrestlers assembled a nice gym and weight program out of old automobile parts they had found in a junkyard. Again, remember the principle. If your athlete believes in it, it will work.

5. *Body weight.* Of course, some really strong athletes don't use any external weights at all. They lift the weight of their own bodies. Most gymnasts rarely lift weights. Such exercises as push-ups, chin-ups, sit-ups, leg lifts, and handstands provide them with all the weight they need. I will talk about age factors later in the section on warnings, but I recommend that you investigate this form of weight training for your young athlete. I simply cannot recommend pumping iron for any person who has not yet grown enough to have a measurable body type—until at least fifteen or sixteen years of age. If your child wants to do strength training before that age, recommend body-weight exercises. That should be as much weight as is needed.

Exercises

Although the Nautilus and Universal exercises are prescribed by the machines themselves, you should know some weight-lifting terms, how the exercises work, and what each develops.

1. *Bench press.* The athlete lies on his back and uses both hands to press the weight suspended just above his face. It is important to lie flat on the bench and to avoid arching the back or trying to push one's legs against the floor. Injuries may occur from doing the exercise incorrectly.

But when the bench press is performed correctly, it should train all the muscles in the arms and shoulders as well as the muscles of the chest and stomach.

2. *Military press.* In the military press, the athlete holds the bar at chin level, and extends the weight to a full arm's length above the head. It is important to keep the back straight through this procedure and to coordinate leg thrusts with arm extension. This not only builds muscles, but it helps with body control. The military press should train the arms, legs, shoulders, and back muscles.

3. *Squats.* In the squat, the athlete puts several pounds on the bar and rests it across the back of the neck. Then, keeping the back straight, the legs are bent and straightened several times. This exercise builds all leg muscles including the thighs and the calves. But it can be very damaging to the knees if it is not done correctly.

4. *Curls.* The athlete takes the weighted bar, holds it in front of him, and curls it up to his chin. In a variation of this, the hands may be reversed on the bar to perform the inverted curl. This exercise trains all muscles of the arms, including those cow-milking muscles we talked about earlier. Oh, the pains of living in the present age!

There are many other exercises. For a specific program, consult your local high-school coach. Most of them have expertise in the area of weight training.

Some Warnings

Strength training is a must for any serious athlete; but like every other good thing, it can be dangerous. Carefully read this list of warnings and do everything you can to help that young athlete get the most out of strength training without getting hurt.

1. Before you let your child start weight training, make sure you both know something about the sport. Weight training is a sophisticated activity. If you cannot talk to the high-school coach, run down to your local sports store and buy a book telling you how to do all the exercises. That is a required investment.

2. Always, always, always have a spotter when anyone is lifting weights. Even the most trained athletes have muscles quit on them in the middle of a lift, and they need help to get rid of the bar. Make sure your child never works out alone.

3. Make sure your child is doing every exercise correctly. An exercise done incorrectly won't do as much good and presents a greater risk of hurting the one who is doing it.

4. Stretching is a vital part of any strength-training program. One must stretch before and afterward. If you don't have time to stretch before you train and after you train on a particular day, don't exercise. By stretching before the program, you warm up the muscles, relax them, and prepare them to develop. By stretching afterward, you keep them from growing bulky and inflexible.

Cardiovascular Training

In addition to building strength, the athlete will want to go through cardiovascular conditioning. Cardiovascular conditioning is preparing the lungs and the heart for the rigors of physical exercise. It requires an activity that speeds up the heartbeat and maintains that pace for several minutes. Since most sports feats last only a short time (running from first to third in baseball, chasing a lob in tennis, running one hundred meters in track, scoring on a fast break in basketball), most games have very little cardiovascular training built into the exercise itself. Thus, the athlete will have to build that kind of training into the practice schedule.

There are several choices: jogging (this is not to be confused with what runners do when they run a marathon in less-than-five-minute miles), walking fast, bicycle riding, long, slow swimming, and cross-country skiing. Out of all these, the very best cardiovascular exercise is the one the person likes enough to do on a regular basis.

I like to jog (not run, jog; there is a big difference). In fact, I like to jog so much that I try to do it every day. If I don't get a chance to jog every day, I miss it enough that I become grumpy. Now, if you had to listen to me talk, you would get the idea that jogging is the only cardiovascular exercise available to the human race. But don't believe it. Cardiovascular exercising is a matter of doing anything physical that will stimulate your heart rate to 150 to 200 percent of its normal rate and hold it there for fifteen or twenty minutes.

If you or your young athlete goes through that procedure at least three times a week, you should get good results. This activity should alter the heart rate a bit, expand the lungs, and stimulate the system so that it would be easier to control weight. All this is necessary for top conditioning. It will help the athlete respond better to aerobic conditioning; it will help to maintain conditioning longer; and it will help in producing a faster recovery from aerobic exhaustion. In fact, many trainers measure athletic condition by checking recovery time. They send the athletes through strenuous aerobic exercises. They then check to see how long it takes the heart rate to return to normal. The athlete who gets there the quickest is in the best condition and should perform better at the end of the contest where victory is often decided.

Anaerobic Training

Cardiovascular exercises take several minutes, but an anaerobic exercise is any one that doesn't last as long as two minutes. This includes most activities in most sports. But for several reasons, any athlete will want to do anaerobic conditioning as well as strength and cardiovascular conditioning. Any good conditioning program includes all parts of the body.

Just as the goal of strength conditioning is strength and the goal of cardiovascular conditioning is endurance, the primary goal of anaerobic conditioning is speed. Even as I say that, however, I am aware that it might be a presumptuous statement. Usually, I am a little cautious of people who propose to take slow people and make them fast. If you really want to do something to guarantee a child can run fast, I suggest you select that child's parents carefully. In spite of all our improvements in both training and analysis, heritage is still the most predictable factor affecting speed. After all, that is the principle behind the racing form one finds at the thoroughbred track.

According to science's best guess, speed is determined by the contraction of some fast-twitch muscle fibers in our bodies. Some people have more of those fast-twitch muscle fibers than others; they probably inherited them.

The theories for improving speed are built around ideas about how to make those muscles contract more quickly. But the athlete has to have the fast-twitch muscle fibers in the first place.

Thus, good speed training must observe two principles. First, the training procedure must come as close as possible to the actual style of running to be used in that sport. I used to coach in small schools where I coached three different sports according to the season. The first few days of each new season were always interesting. When football season was over, our players knew they were in top physical condition, but they almost died when they began training for basketball. They had to become acclimated to the new type of anaerobic movement demanded by each different sport.

Actually, anaerobic activities can be a part of any good workout. The baseball player can work on conditioning while running the bases as fast as possible. The tennis player can practice going to the net and retracing to the backline as fast as possible. The basketball player can practice the half-court fast break. The football player can run ten yards, get down, and run again. These exercises not only achieve the anaerobic training requirements, but they also help the athlete practice gamelike skills.

The second principle of speed training is that the speed or quickness is often a matter of form. If your young athlete needs to improve speed, he or she needs to work out under the watchful supervision of a coach who knows something about form. If a young person develops a bad habit in running form, it may be tough to correct that habit as the child grows and the need for more speed increases.

The experts are now finding that anaerobic training may have even greater effect and possibilities than what we have always believed. Richard H. Dominguez, M.D. and Robert Gajda, in their book *Total Body Training,* * discuss some ideas that are different from what has been believed in the past about prevention and rehabilitation of injuries. We concur with these two authorities in their findings. They believe that anaerobics are important in rehabilitating injuries and training athletes. They make the following statements.

1. Anaerobic training causes an increase in strength in the muscles and tendons.
2. Anaerobic training creates an increase in flexibility.
3. Anaerobic training increases circulation.
4. Anaerobic training improves the stability and strength of the joints.
5. Anaerobic training increases muscles, anaerobic function, and ability to do anaerobic activities.
6. Anaerobic training increases the percentage of fast-twitch fiber in muscles.

*Richard H. Dominguez and Robert J. Gajda, *Total Body Training* (New York: Warner Books, 1983).

7. Anaerobic training increases the ability to store more glycogen for energy.

Stretching

I have already mentioned that stretching is a vital part of any conditioning program. If you want to teach your child something essential to athletic growth and potential, teach proper stretching techniques. This will help in learning how to prepare for conditioning; it will help to make the most of conditioning and will help to reduce the risk of injuries. The important word here is *proper*. Like other exercises, proper stretching is a good procedure. Improper stretching could be damaging.

Again, out of all the ones available, the best stretching program is the one your child believes in enough to do. Stretching is a process of warming and relaxing muscles before the athlete puts tension and pressure on them. Any stretching program that reaches all the muscles is a good one. The following exercises are general and are no better or worse than any other exercises. Athletes in specific sports may need to use another set of muscles and may need a different stretching routine.

1. *Jogging.* We recommend that every athlete begin every workout with about five minutes of very slow jogging. This warms the body and relaxes the muscles.

2. *The gradual principle.* Some athletes stretch by going through a whole series of normal training exercises, but they begin very slowly and work gradually into full range of motion. These athletes maintain that these exercises are good for them because the exercises are the very same ones the athlete will need in the practice or contest. Thus, the athlete is warming up and stretching the exact muscles that will be used during the event itself.

3. *Body weight.* Some athletes use some simple body weight exercises to stretch prior to and after strenuous exercise. Chin-ups stretch the arm, shoulder, and back muscles; sit-ups stretch the stomach and back muscles; and push-ups stretch the arm muscles. According to these athletes, these exercises performed slowly give them enough stretching to let them move into the activity.

4. *Standard stretches.* On the other hand, some athletes use a highly developed set of exercises designed especially for the purpose of stretching prior to the activity. There are probably several hundred of these. If you have a chance to go to a professional game of almost any sport, try to go a little early and watch what the pros do. You will see many different

stretching approaches and exercises. Let me describe some of the more common ones.

a. Hurdlers' stretch: The athlete sits down with one leg extended full in front and the other curled back. As he points his toe of the extended foot, he stretches the hamstring and calf muscles. As he bends forward, he continues to work on the hamstring but adds back and stomach muscles. If he leans back, he adds even more pressure to those muscles he is stretching. Of course, he will need to alternate feet during the exercise.

Although this exercise is popular among many coaches and athletes, other coaches have some reservations about it. You may want to check with your high-school coach about this.

b. The butterfly: The athlete sits down and puts both feet out in front, then pushes the legs apart with the elbows, thus stretching the groin muscles. One can also bend forward in this position.

c. The crossover: Standing, the athlete crosses one leg over the other, then holding both legs straight, bends down as far as possible. This stretches the muscles of the legs, particularly in the backs of the legs.

d. The arm rotation: The athlete stands with feet together and extends the arms fully out to the sides. This warms up and stretches the arm and shoulder muscles.

e. The arms behind the back: Standing, the athlete locks hands behind his back. He pulls the arms up as high as he can. Baseball players frequently use a bat behind the back.

f. The neck push: The athlete pushes his head against an immovable object. This gets the neck muscles to work. He can then rotate his head.

g. The jumping jack: This is a good exercise to conclude the set. By swinging the arms above the head and jumping at the same time, the athlete employs all the warmed muscles and makes them all work in coordination.

I pause here to remind you again that this chapter is very general. I am only trying to acquaint you with some general terms. This matter is too complex to be covered in a few pages. My goal has been to make you aware of the need for conditioning. But you need more information. If your child is in athletics, you will want to get expert advice from a coach, a trainer, or at least a book.

Now that we have convinced you of the need for strenuous conditioning and training, I am going to propose another vital component to both mental and physical conditioning, that is, rest. Rest isn't a contradiction of what I have proposed. It is a necessary component.

Rest

Your child has been playing or participating in a sport for three to four years and seems to love it, excels to some degree, and doesn't complain about practices. The child is old enough to begin to make some individual choices. You've discussed participating in sport, talked about interest in other activities, and the signal is go.

How can you help protect your child from self-burnout? *Burnout* is this generation's term for doing the same thing too often and for too long a time. Burnout means that the activity is controlling the person's life instead of the person's controlling the activity.

Everyone needs to take a break or vacation from practicing, drilling, and training—especially after months of hard training and just previous to the main event. Allow time for the break and then pick up the practice and drill routine just prior to the season or event.

An illustration that comes to mind is of Jim who is a star player because of his intelligence about the game, his continual determination, practice, and drill, and his high percentage of natural talent. For years, Jim's goal has been to play with the team. He has done exercises to build quickness; he has lifted weights; he has tried to eat nutritional foods; he has attended clinics; and most of all, he has continued to practice and drill all year.

One August, I was talking with Jim. I suggested that he rest for two weeks since he had not missed a day of drills other than Sundays since the last season. He didn't take my advice, and by the middle of the season, he admitted he was tired of the game. All that work was bringing him enough success that he wanted to play, and he certainly enjoyed the games and winning—but he was tired. From then on it took mental determination to keep him going. It would have been better to have rested the mind and body for a little while previous to regular sports practice.

If your child participates in two or three sports, periods of rest are important. If there can be no rest between one sport and the next—football season ends on Friday night and basketball tryouts start on Monday night—try to give your child mental rest by not discussing in detail either sport for awhile. Of course, show an interest, but leave goal setting and other serious discussions for later.

Don't forget! Rest is as vital to the conditioning program as exercise.

What Parents Ask

1. *My thirteen-year-old son wants a set of weights to build himself up for football. Should I buy them for him?*

   No! Not yet. First, go down to a sports store and buy a good book on weight training. Then consult an expert—your local high-school coach or a trainer. No young person should begin weights until he knows what he is doing. Weights can be harmful if they are not handled correctly.

2. *How hard should an athlete push himself during workouts?*

   That depends on several factors—how seasoned the athlete is; how often he works out; the purpose of the workout. One of the great joys of sports is the joy of discovery; of discovering that one can run faster, jump higher, throw farther than one ever thought possible. This is one of the purposes of practice. The most successful basketball coach I know has an interesting theory. His practices are only two hours long, but they are always full speed. He never allows players to loaf in the gym. That way, his players never loaf in games (or seldom ever).

3. *My daughter loves to play tennis, but she hates to condition. What should I do?*

   Actually, she may be getting enough conditioning just from playing. If not, help her create some gamelike exercises. That way, she will be practicing her sport while she is conditioning. If you want to check her progress, check her resting pulse rate. Then check her pulse rate after she has played a tough match. Then check to see how long it takes the pulse to return to normal. If she is reducing her recovery time, she is probably making progress in conditioning.

11. *Injuries*

I have never heard of a child falling off a chair and breaking an arm while watching television. Children do get hurt, but usually the more active ones are more likely to get hurt than those who spend most of their time sitting. Since sports involve activity, children in sports (and adults as well) stand a greater chance of incurring an occasional pain. If you have an athlete at your house, you need to understand something about pain. You need to understand something about sports injuries.

To be honest, if you have an athlete at your house, you need to understand far more about injuries than I am going to tell you in this chapter. I am not telling you this to frighten you. Your knowing something about injuries will give you some peace of mind. You may never need to doctor a sports injury; but in case you do, you will be ready. And your being ready to take care of an injury should give your athlete a comforting sense, too.

I recommend as strongly as I can that you make a measly investment of about five bucks (less than a ticket to a good football game) to buy a good book on sports injuries. *The Complete Book of Sports Medicine* by Dr. Richard Dominguez is one of the best books I know of. The author is a doctor, so he understands the body; but he is also the parent of some young athletes, so he understands children in sports. And everything in the book is arranged for use as a resource tool.

I repeat. If your child is going to participate in sports, care enough to purchase a book on sports injuries. Since I am going to trust you to do that, I can use the rest of this chapter to make a few observations from the point of view of a parent who learned a few things from coaching.

Pain

I am not sure I know what pain is or what causes it, but there seems to be a lot of pain in sports. Some of this is necessary, but some of it isn't. Conditioning itself is never a pain-free enterprise. If either you or your teenage daughter asks a bunch of muscles to rise up and go to work in active sports, those muscles will complain about the change in status. Activity makes the body tired, and a tired body hurts. Growing children sometimes feel pain just through the natural process of growing. And life, particularly the sports life, is filled with nicks, bruises, bumps, and small sprains.

Your problem as a parent is to decide how much of this pain is necessary and when the pain is serious enough to merit immediate attention, such as a doctor's care or even a trip to the emergency room.

I can't offer you any real suggestions to make your parental task any easier, but maybe I can offer you some comfort. Unless you own an x-ray machine and a medical diploma, you may never know how to evaluate the extent of your child's pain. A couple of years ago, we delayed a football game nearly forty-five minutes in freezing rain to splint a player's mangled leg and rush him to the hospital. We didn't know what was wrong with that fellow's leg, but we knew it was serious. Yet, when we went back into the dressing room at halftime, there he was taking a shower. Apparently, we had missed on our evaluation of the damage.

A few years ago, a young man came to me during practice. He had some discoloration in the back of his hand, but he wasn't feeling any pain. We put ice on the hand for a few minutes and sent him back into the practice fray. After practice, I suggested an x-ray, just to be on the safe side. He had a broken bone and had to wear the ugliest cast I have ever seen.

Even those of us who spend most of our time around sports often get fooled. Don't be embarrassed. If there is any question, consult an expert—either a doctor or a sports trainer. If the injury is serious enough to need treatment, you will know that you have done the right thing. If it isn't, you will join a large club of those of us who have misevaluated pain once or twice.

The Physical

In my playing days, and even when I was a young coach, I often looked at that preseason sports physical as something of a necessary nuisance. But after twenty-five years of coaching and gathering stories, I no longer view it that casually. A thorough physical examination is vitally important, and no person of any age should be permitted into organized sports activity without one.

Although the names and details vary, the story is the same. Some perfectly healthy-looking young person wants to participate in sports, so he or she trots down to the family doctor to have an innocent-looking form filled out. But in a routine examination, the doctor finds a potentially dangerous problem: a misaligned back, a weak muscle, a deformed joint, a heart problem. Sometimes, the problem is so minor that it can be corrected with a special shoe or pad or medicine. Sometimes the problem requires surgery. Sometimes the young person can't participate in sports anymore for fear of his very life. But whatever the result, thank God for the sports physical.

If your child is going to participate in sports, insist on that physical at least yearly. If the club or organization doesn't require it or if the program requires only something minor, take your child in yourself. Insist that the doctor give a thorough examination. Make sure the doctor knows that this is a sports physical so such things as muscles and bones can be checked. Insist that the doctor check the heart both before and after exercise.

Condition

Since we have already devoted a whole chapter to condition, I won't repeat anything here except to say that a conditioned athlete is less likely to get hurt than an unconditioned one. An athlete who knows the rules and is confident about being able to play is less likely to get hurt than one who is indecisive. An athlete who plays hard is less likely to get hurt than one who loafs.

Most school-run programs recognize this and require preseasoning conditioning programs before the athletes can take part in game situations. If your child is in a program that has no requirement, make such a program a family requirement. In fact, it wouldn't hurt you to go out with your teenage daughter for some early morning jogs a few weeks before basketball season starts.

Equipment

In all my coaching experiences in several different sports, the two injuries that have been most common and the most costly in player time are blisters and viral infections. (Okay, viral infections aren't really injuries, but they do incapacitate a player like any other injury, and some of them are sports related.) The problem is that both of these injuries are often caused by faulty equipment. They could be prevented with some common sense in handling equipment.

The worst problem is a piece of equipment that doesn't fit. My best basketball player comes to those hard first practices still wearing last year's shoes. Of course, her feet have grown. She is a growing girl and everything has grown. But she pinches her toes into those shoes and tries to make it until the end of the month before she buys new ones. But then the blisters pop up. If we are careful, and she doesn't get an infection, we lose her for only about three days. Then she hobbles gingerly through three more weeks of practice and the first two games. All that could have been prevented.

The football player's pants are only slightly too large—no big deal. He can just pull his belt in at the waist and make them work. But then his thigh pads slip around to the side of his legs and he gets a deep bruise from a blow that should have hit the pad. This could have been prevented.

The second problem is equipment that gets dirty and stays dirty too long. I have no idea why some young people have such an aversion to clean sports equipment. I have seen sweat socks and supporters that were on the verge of coming to life with thousands of microscopic critters living on two months of collected sweat and crud. This, too, is dangerous.

Sports put young people in such close contact with each other that there is always the risk of spreading diseases: athlete's foot, rashes, boils, colds, mononucleosis. There is no need to contribute to the risk by wearing filthy clothes and equipment. Insist that your child bring equipment home to be washed regularly. You will help reduce the risk of infection, and you will help me make our dressing room smell better.

Outfitting your young athlete is an important part of participation. Make sure your child always has equipment that fits and is clean. You don't need to spend a vast amount of money on equipment, but you do need to make sure it is good enough to provide the best possible protection. If you have any questions, ask coaches or read the magazines on that sport. Often the most expensive equipment is not necessarily the best. Unless you know your sports equipment dealer personally, he may try to sell you the most expensive item. Consult someone before you buy.

Incidentally, don't worry about asking coaches, even if you don't know any. Call the local high school and ask to speak to the coach in that sport. We coaches love to give advice. We really like to think we are experts, so your call will contribute to our self-image.

Time

I don't know much about what makes injuries heal, but I do know that most of them require a good dose of time. Despite all the great advances we have made in the medical field, the healing process still takes time. If your athlete gets injured, you, the parent, must understand that time factor.

You must insist that your child takes the time necessary to heal sufficiently to be able to return without risk of reinjury. This may be a lonely position. You may not get much help from the coach, from the other players, or from your child. But do insist.

At the same time, understand what your child as an injured athlete is going through. When playing, your child was a part of something. The coaches and other players paid attention, involved your child in the planning and the activities. Sports participation was an outlet for frustrations and energy. Now that there has been an injury, those frustrations and energy are still there, but they are even stronger because your child is no longer a part of something.

As a coach, I must confess that regardless of how hard we try to include that injured player into all team decisions and activities, we never get the job done, not totally. That injured player is always an outsider. We coaches and fellow players don't have as much time for an injured athlete.

As a parent, you must understand this. An injured athlete is a lonely creature. When your athlete gets injured, do whatever it takes to fill that void. If you are good at doing that, perhaps you will be able to convince your child to take the time needed to heal.

The Parents' Perspective

Several years ago, my best high-school basketball player fractured a small bone at the base of his thumb. It was no big deal, just a small, hairline fracture that caused very little pain. I could have taped up his whole thumb with six cents worth of tape, and he could have scored twenty-five points a game for us. And we needed those twenty-five points. But the fracture was U-shaped. If he bumped his thumb again and fractured it across that unbroken part, the chip could have fallen out and the thumb would have been stiff for life. Of course, the young man wanted to take the risk. Youth is always impetuously indestructible. I was hesitant, but, oh, how we needed those twenty-five points per game. The parents settled it. They said, "No, absolutely not." And our best basketball player didn't play that season because of a hairline fracture in his thumb. The community caused a minor war. A self-appointed delegation went to see the parents. Old friends quit speaking to one another, and everyone treated me as if I were an alien to blame.

Of course, without our star, we didn't have much of a season, and that didn't help matters much. But I survived. Our players survived. And believe it or not, the town survived. It is still there.

That young man is now one of the best-known oral surgeons in that part of the country. In fact, I am planning to see him in a few months for a root canal job. I am sure happy his thumb works.

Liquids

Athletes sweat. More liquids pass through an active child's body than through an inactive child's body. If you have an athlete at your house, help prevent injuries by providing plenty of liquids. Dehydration can lead to serious problems. Make sure your child understands enough about the topic to take in enough liquids. The running experts tell us that if we get thirsty we have already begun to dehydrate. Thus, they recommend that we drink even before we get thirsty.

Most coaches, even football coaches, understand that now and provide enough water for the athletes during practice and games. If your child's coach doesn't understand that, remind him or her. You may be helping your child prevent injuries.

Emergencies

All right, you have taken all the preventive measures including prayer, and your athlete still gets hurt. What do you do? I have three simple but serious suggestions.

1. Don't panic. Don't be in so big a hurry to do something that you

do the wrong thing. Slow down. Talk to the child. Keep your head. Think clearly.

2. Don't ever help an injured person up. If an injured player is down, wait until the player is ready to get up alone. You may think that is cruel, but if the player is hurt too badly to get up alone, you might complicate things by helping. If it is possible to get up alone, the player probably won't be further injured. Incidentally, I use that same principle when I see an older person fall on the street.

3. Use ice. Whatever the injury is, you can almost always start with ice. Ice is a good emergency treatment for many injuries such as breaks, bruises, sprains, and tears. Apply it immediately. If ice won't help it, at least it won't hurt anything; and it will give you enough time to get your child to the doctor, or at least look up the problem in that sports medicine book you bought just for this purpose.

What Parents Ask

1. *How do I know when an injury is bad enough to merit a doctor's care?*

   Use common sense and prayer, and don't take any chances. Sure, you can tell about some things, but don't worry about embarrassing yourself before the doctor. If you make a mistake, err in being too cautious.

2. *How do I pay all those doctor bills if my child does get injured in sports?*

   Buy insurance. I repeat. Buy insurance. Unless your income is a whole lot higher than mine, you simply can't afford to have your child participate in any organized sport without insurance. Usually the special sports plans are relatively inexpensive. Ask an insurance person or the principal at school.

3. *My son wants to play football, but I am so afraid of his getting hurt. What do I do?*

   I won't lie to you. Some football players do get hurt. Some don't. We can never predict which one will. Fortunately, almost all injuries do heal. Now ask yourself, "If my son doesn't play football, what will he do with that extra time? How will he develop his self-image and social position?" Sometimes the alternatives to football are more dangerous than football itself.

12. *Food for Athletes*

I have always wanted to write a diet book. That seems to be a sure road to instant fame and success. And I could really pack the material into a book on how to feed an athlete. I could cite a mass of scientific details about what is in various foods, particularly some bizarre and exotic things; and I could tell how all those chemicals and components make the body grow strong and fast. Then I could quote that always sincere testimony of some great athlete who attributes all his success to my secret magic diet plan.

That would be an easy book to write, and such a volume would make your work as a parent a great deal easier. You could whip out those menus, serve up that food, and all of a sudden your flesh and blood would be going for the gold in the next Olympics.

Unfortunately, it isn't that simple. What is even more unfortunate is that I can't even be very persuasive in prescribing a magic diet for athletes.

I realize that there are some good books on that very subject, and I don't want to discredit the books or the authors or their theories. I also realize that there are good foods and bad foods. But all of these great scientific facts and formulas come with a warning, a delightful warning: Not all human bodies work the same way all the time. Isn't that nice to know?

Every year at our college we have an athlete who wants to gain weight. As far as we know, this young athlete, male or female, is in perfect health and excellent condition. He or she just wants to add a few pounds to pack a little more force in football or basketball or field hockey. The athlete goes on a special diet, but after eating five times a day, drinking three milk shakes, taking special weight pills, and eating donuts for a late-night snack, not a pound is gained. But we have this other athlete who gains five pounds just dreaming about food. What's the difference?

I don't know, and I am glad I don't know. If such things as food, weight, and human bodies were exact sciences, we wouldn't need the game. We could just plug all the pertinent information into a computer, and it would tell us who won and by how much. It might be more predictable, but it wouldn't be as much fun. That is why feeding an athlete is fun. You may make some educated guesses about what is good for your athlete, but you will never know for sure how well it will work until after the performance.

If it is all so chancy anyway, how then do you feed an athlete on a day-by-day basis? Why, that is easy. You feed an athlete the same way you would feed any other child. You know food. You have read diet books and cookbooks. You know how to feed your family. Feed your athlete by using the same common sense you would use for feeding any other child.

Be careful about that last paragraph. I have just said something controversial, but I hope I said it so subtly you won't notice it and tell your child's coach. Some coaches might suggest a special treatment for some athletes. They might suggest, for example, that you put your healthy thirteen-year-old wrestler on a crash diet so he will make weight class for the next meet. Or the football coach might suggest that you try to plump up your fourteen-year-old so he will be a little heavier for next season. Or the gymnastics coach might suggest a severe diet for your puberty-age daughter to hold off her natural development as long as possible.

We, the authors of this book (and thorough-going coaches), cannot agree with any of those positions. We recommend as firmly as we know how that you feed your growing child a normal, healthy, steady diet, and that you make no special provisions for weight gain or loss unless those provisions have been prescribed by a doctor. Physical growth is a part of God's wonderful scheme for all of us, and we simply don't do our children any favors by contradicting those normal patterns, so long as the child is healthy. No sport, no event, no season, no coach is ever worth your taking a chance with your child's natural growth pattern.

Of course, your athlete will definitely need to eat regularly. However, because practice and game schedules often destroy family routines, you may find it difficult to schedule those family meals on a regular plan. And there are some special occasions that require special consideration. One of those is the pregame meal.

Since the proper pregame meal is not a totally scientific affair, you will need to consider both your child's specific diet needs and the nature of the contest itself. Preparing to run a fifty-meter dash in a local track meet is different from preparing to run a twenty-six-mile marathon. You will want to feed your athlete appropriately. But the principle is probably the same, regardless of the contest. In preparing your child for any athletic contest, you don't want to load down the digestive system and make it work overtime while all the other parts of the body need that blood and energy for the contest itself. In other words, in the pregame meal, you want to feed your child foods that are easy to digest, and you want to stay away from those that are more difficult to digest.

That is a simple principle, but deciding exactly how to follow it has been fun over the past twenty-five years. The experts have changed their minds about fifty times. For the purpose of providing you the best information I can, I will report what the experts are saying this year. If they change their minds next year, I will write this chapter again.

Presently, a good pregame meal would consist of such foods as pancakes, fruit, soft drinks, spaghetti or other forms of pasta or maybe even a candy bar. These foods are supposed to be easy to digest, and the stuff of these foods is more quickly turned into the energy that the athlete needs during the contest. On the other hand, foods like red meat (steak, ham) and milk are harder to digest and are slower to produce the energy they afford.

About five years ago, most of the coaches of the various sports at our college decided to change from the traditional pregame meal of steak and potatoes to the suggested meal of pancakes, fruit cocktail, and Coke. We now try to feed this to our athletes about three or four hours before the game. Although we don't designate the quantity any athlete eats, we do suggest that each quits before getting stuffed. So far, we have only noticed two small problems. Our athletes would really rather have steak and potatoes, so they gripe about the pregame meal. And most of the athletes are really hungry by the time the game is over, so we have to get them to food quickly or face a possible revolt.

As I said earlier, feeding an athlete is fun. But having an athlete at your house is fun, too. With common sense and a good sense of humor, you should be able to survive and perhaps even enjoy both ordeals.

What Parents Ask

1. *My fourteen-year-old son plays football. His coach is urging him to gain weight for next season. What do you suggest?*

   Get another coach! I am really mostly serious. If your son is eating a balanced diet, if he is healthy, and if he works hard enough to keep in condition, he probably weighs what nature wants him to weigh. Why mess with that?

2. *Should an athlete eat differently during season than in off-season?*

   Not necessarily. This fast-and-famine idea is not very healthy for growing children.

3. *My daughter is overweight, but she just can't diet. Would active participation in a sport help her control her weight?*

   Yes, it could have direct bearing. With proper exercise, we are in a better position to use our food. But her participation could also have a big indirect effect. If your daughter really develops an interest in sports and makes a commitment, she will begin to take charge of her body, to discipline herself. Often this carries over to diet. Frequently, as a college football coach, I suggest to some player that he should lose a few pounds. Almost every player has enough commitment to football that he can control his impulse to overeat and lose the weight I suggest.

PART FOUR
Sports Opportunities

13. *Surveying the Sports*

Now that you have weighed the advantages and disadvantages of organized sports participation to your child and to your family, and you and your child have made a decision to participate, you now have to decide together which sport or sports are best for your little athlete and for you. Actually, you are probably in the best position to lend your child advice because you know your child better than anyone else. You know your child's personality and history so you can make some predictions about what kind of body will result when all the growth processes and spurts are finished.

Since picking the right sport or sports can become a rather important decision as your child grows, you need to make sure both you and your child have considered all the possibilities before you make that decision. To help you, I have compiled a brief digest of the most common sports opportunities. To simplify this process, I have further divided the sports into two categories: team sports and individual sports. Team sports include baseball and softball, basketball, football, soccer, volleyball, and hockey. Individual sports include wrestling, track, swimming, gymnastics, golf, and tennis.

Team Sports

Baseball and Softball

1. *Opportunities.* A child can start this sport as young as five or six years of age through park-district and youth programs, and can continue to play through slow pitch games in retirement villages. At the youngest age, the game is frequently T-ball, where the child hits a ball set upon a T-stand rather than a pitched ball. From this beginning, there are ample

opportunities for boys and girls to continue to play through various programs including school and park-district programs. There is probably more opportunity to play baseball or softball at the lower levels than any other sport. Any child who wants to play can almost always find an opportunity. Baseball is also a good game for the informal, backyard approach, and this gives the interested child one more opportunity.

2. *Physical characteristics.* Baseball and softball are sports that can utilize athletes of almost any size as long as they are strong enough to perform some basic physical movements. Probably the biggest physical demand is on hand and eye coordination, but speed in running and quickness in short movements are also assets. Because of the variety of the positions, however, a child who is big and slow can find an appropriate position, just as the smaller, quicker child can.

3. *Mental characteristics.* The beginner should show enough interest to want to learn the rules of the sport. Although baseball is a noncontact sport, the child needs to accept the challenge of doing the job. In specific moments, the baseball player is isolated and in full view of teammates and the crowd, but the individual feats are still performed for the benefit of the team. Even though this is a slow-moving sport, at least to the spectators, it requires constant mental alertness. The good player is always planning ahead about what to do should a given possibility occur. Anticipating these possibilities is a part of baseball savvy—knowing what to do when the time comes.

4. *Costs.* Basic costs would include a glove, shoes, and maybe a bat; the other costs of the sport are usually absorbed by the sponsoring agencies. A child who is careful with that equipment could probably play for a few years with one small investment.

5. *Injuries.* Anytime children are active, they are more likely to encounter small injuries. But beyond this, baseball is relatively safe. Some potential hazards can be greatly reduced if the athletes take proper precautions. Although there is always a possibility of getting hit with a ball, the risk of injury is reduced when the child wears a helmet. By the same reasoning, players can avoid the serious possibility of getting hit with a bat if they just take some precautions. If your child plays baseball or softball, you can help by stressing those precautions. Although such accidents are rare, a baseball injury can be very serious.

Basketball

1. *Opportunities.* Since basketball requires raw strength and height,

children usually don't begin the game in an organized environment until they are at least ten or eleven years of age. But after that, there is almost equal opportunity for boys and girls. Many elementary schools run low-competition basketball programs for their students, and there are other programs through park districts, boys' clubs, YMCAs and YWCAs. But since this sport requires a gym, opportunities in basketball are more limited than some other sports which are more portable.

The limited number of players on a team constitutes another problem. School programs from junior high on can usually only use fewer than twenty players. Everyone else will be denied the opportunity to participate unless those people participate in the intramural basketball program open to everybody. But intramural programs will never provide the young athlete with the structure, the coaching, or even the practice that varsity competition provides.

Although modified versions of basketball can be adapted to the backyard, most structured opportunities for play after graduation from school are limited to town teams and amateur programs for players in their twenties.

2. *Physical characteristics.* Although basketball can use a few short players if they are very quick, the emphasis is always on height. If your son has inherited the possibility of being taller than six two as an adult, he will have a good chance in the sport. On the other hand, if he doesn't have any chance of being that tall, and if he doesn't seem to be particularly quick with hands and feet, you may want to lend your support to another sport.

3. *Mental characteristics.* Although basketball can be rough at times, it is designed to be a noncontact sport. It is one of the finesse games. Good players usually have themselves under emotional control because the game does require constant alertness and quick thinking. Despite the many patterns that make basketball a science, most of the game is still as versatile as the bounce of the ball.

4. *Costs.* Basketball can be a relatively inexpensive sport if someone else is paying for the gym time. In this case, the player may be asked to buy a pair of shoes and socks. Of course, if you want to provide your child the best opportunity, you will want to put up a goal in the backyard and buy an outdoor basketball, but even those aren't too expensive. On the other hand, if your child is not playing in a school program—either varsity or intramurals—he or she might be expected to pay some of the gym costs, and that could be expensive.

5. *Injuries.* If you have a basketball player at your house, learn all you can about doctoring blisters. You will have a chance to use your medical knowledge. These are as common as dribbles. You may also want to take special precautions against colds. Because basketball is most often played in the winter season, the players get hot and sweaty in a gym and then go outside before they have readjusted to the climate. Buy your child a stocking cap to wear to and from practice and games, and make sure your child gets plenty of vitamin C.

In the early adolescent years, when your child is going through some growth spurts, some shin splints may result from running on the gym floors. These may be more common in girls than in boys, but in either case they are a painful nuisance.

Other than a few odd ones, basketball has been almost free of serious injuries. An added advantage is that the game requires constant movement, so it does contribute to a child's physical condition.

Football

1. *Opportunities.* First, we have to accept the fact that football is a game for boys. Very few girls play much football other than in isolated powderpuff games that are scheduled as fun and novelty events. However, most towns now have some kind of park-district or certified program for boys beginning at eight or nine years of age. At the junior-high and high-school levels, the opportunities are almost unlimited. There are more people playing football than any other school-sponsored sport in this country. Since football needs such a large number of people for practices and games, schools usually don't cut football players, so in theory the program is open to any boy who wants to participate.

Of course, football is a game for *young* men, and there are very few opportunities to play organized tackle football after college. In fact, we authors coach small-college football, so each year at the last game of the season we give special recognition to our seniors who are putting on football gear for the last time in their lives.

2. *Physical characteristics.* Although there are a few small people in the game, football is primarily a contest between big people with brute strength. In fact, most high-school, college, and even professional players lift weights to pump up their muscles until they are through with their careers. If your son has the potential, the frame, and the heritage to develop bulk, he could find a place in football regardless of his speed. However, if he is likely to be smaller than his peers, you may want to

help him learn to like some other activity where his size won't be such a disadvantage.

3. *Mental characteristics.* Football is a contact sport. People who play must enjoy bumping into one another. Although those stories of mayhem and brutality may be exaggerated, particularly for the television audience, football is a rough sport. The appropriate question may be, "Why do people want to play? What is the attraction?"

Maybe the attraction for many players is the roughness itself. There is a rather common urge in young people to take risks. Not only is there a certain daring about it, but taking a risk helps them prove that they have courage. Risks make life exciting and romantic.

When I was young I used to ride down the big hill curled up inside a barrel. I hated that ride. Everytime I went, I got dizzy and bruised. But I went regularly. Now that I am older, I don't need that kind of thrill anymore, nor the thrill of riding a roller coaster or driving fast or playing football. But some boys do; and for them, football is a wholesome and fairly safe outlet for that need to take a risk. If your son is the kind of person who needs that kind of risk, think seriously before you deny him the opportunity to play football.

Football takes discipline and the will to continue when one doesn't feel like it. For this reason, football is good training for any rigorous lifestyle. Also, for most players, a football play requires a specific maneuver, so football players are not asked to make those quick judgments and decisions as often as basketball players. But they are asked to follow instructions to the letter.

4. *Costs.* A football uniform is expensive. In most school situations, the school buys the gear except for shoes, socks, and maybe a mouthpiece. But in some of the park-district programs, the players may be asked to furnish pads and helmets. In this case, you ought to outfit your son in the very best. If you can't afford the best, then he is running a greater risk when he plays.

The second major cost of football is insurance. Never let your son play without having adequate coverage. Take the advice of coaches. Even during the safest drills, players still break their fingers, fall on the ground and separate their shoulders, tear up their knees, or lose their contacts. You need to cover yourself.

5. *Injuries.* This discussion leads to an obvious fact. Sons get hurt playing football. Your son may play for fifteen years and never suffer so much as a broken fingernail, but there is no guarantee. Although mod-

ern training methods and equipment have done a lot to lessen some of the injuries, and really serious injuries are very rare, there are always broken bones, bruises, abrasions, and sore knuckles.

As a parent, you must seriously consider why your son wants to play football. Don't pass this off as a boyish whim. He may really need the activity. If he does, football is a lot safer than driving an automobile seventy miles per hour, skateboarding in the middle of the street, jumping over a garbage can, sniffing airplane glue, or getting drunk on Saturday night.

Soccer

1. *Opportunities.* Although soccer is the most popular sport in the world, it is still in its growing stages in the United States. Its popularity with both players and fans increases every year, and the opportunities increase also. There are several reasons for this. The sport is inexpensive. It can fit into a couple of different times during the year. It can be played proficiently by girls and boys. Young children can play soccer earlier than many other sports, including baseball. The game requires several players so there is more opportunity to participate. And the sport offers good conditioning.

Across the nation, park-district programs for smaller children are expanding every year, and junior high and high schools are adding programs as rapidly as they can find qualified coaches. Soccer is probably the fastest growing sport in this country presently, and it looks as if it will continue to grow. Although the sport may never become as popular as the three traditional games of football, basketball, and baseball, it will attract a large number of participants and fans. Unlike football, it also offers some opportunity for people to play after college.

2. *Physical characteristics.* Good soccer players need to be fast. In a normal soccer game, there are hundreds of footraces. It helps to be quick and have good control of feet and body, and it helps to have a strong leg, but those things can be learned. The raw ability is speed. Size is not that important.

3. *Mental characteristics.* Soccer players need to enjoy running and moving. They need to react quickly to situations and to stay alert. They need to have the will to drive themselves, to reach down into themselves and run faster than they thought they could. But they also need to know how to respond to frustration. Soccer is a strange game because there is always more offense than scoring. A player who has kicked a soccer ball

all the way down the field just to have the goalie block the shot in the last instant is about as frustrated as the guy who had to push the pebble up the hill only to have it roll to the bottom each time he almost reached the crest. A good soccer player must bounce back from that kind of frustration and keep at it until the ball does get into the goal.

Soccer also is an excellent sport to teach teamwork and cooperation. It takes everybody to share in the victory.

4. *Costs.* Probably one of the reasons soccer is so popular around the world is that it is so inexpensive. All the children need is a field and a ball. Of course, you can buy your child a nice pair of shoes, but other than that, there is little expense.

5. *Injuries.* Anytime athletes have to make quick starts, stops, and body adjustments, they run the risk of muscle pulls, which may be the most common soccer injury for players who have already developed muscle definition in their legs. Other than that, soccer players do get a few sprains and twists, and, occasionally, body contact can leave bruises or even a rare break.

Volleyball

1. *Opportunities.* Although volleyball is becoming more popular and it drew large crowds in the 1984 Olympics, the opportunities for the average child are rather limited. Volleyball is not a sport easily mastered by younger children. Some junior high schools have programs, but the game really doesn't come into its own until high school. Several state-school associations have now added volleyball to their programs. Some of these are for girls only, but there are some boys' programs and even some mixed programs. Opportunities for organized participation may be limited, but unorganized opportunities are everywhere—in playgrounds, on beaches, in backyards, and in the middle of quiet streets. Thus, this sport does offer people an opportunity to continue even after they have grown too old for some other team sports.

2. *Physical characteristics.* Size is not much of a factor, but the good volleyball player must have natural spring or jumping ability and body control while in the air. This is a difficult form of coordination. Good hand and eye coordination and strong wrists are also needed, as well as the ability to use both hands.

3. *Mental characteristics.* Since volleyball is a noncontact sport, it is a game that can be enjoyed and mastered by the more passive athlete. It is a game of skill and finesse rather than intensity or strength. Like a good

soccer player, the good volleyball player must be able to respond to frustration.

4. *Costs.* Because of its flexibility, volleyball is very portable and inexpensive. Even the most structured programs won't require much more than a pair of shoes.

5. *Injuries.* Fingers are the most common victims, but young adolescents may also be prone to shin splints or blisters from all that jumping.

Hockey

1. *Opportunities.* For the most part, hockey is a regional sport. It isn't very popular south of the Mason-Dixon line. In fact, it isn't all that popular south of the Great Lakes states. But in the areas where the game is an established sport, it is both a popular fan sport and a good opportunity for boys from six years old through college age.

2. *Physical characteristics.* Obviously, hockey first requires an ability to skate, which requires balance and coordination. After that, good hockey players know how to make an asset out of quickness and size. A strong wrist comes in handy, too.

3. *Mental characteristics.* Like football, hockey is a contact sport. Although it is a ball and stick game with emphasis on hand and eye coordination, it is also a very physical activity. Good players enjoy bumping into people. Since this is one of the fastest sports, hockey requires constant alertness and quick thinking and reactions. The good player must have a knowledge of the overall aspects of the sport (savvy), and he must plan ahead and anticipate. This makes hockey something of an unusual sport. It has both the physical demands of football and the mental demands of basketball.

4. *Costs.* In the areas of the country cold enough to construct outdoor facilities, hockey is not terribly expensive. It does require skates, special padded uniforms, and the breakable sticks. But in the areas not cold enough for outdoor rinks, those indoor facilities are expensive in both time and money. Somebody has to pay rink time; but even when an organization pays instead of the individual players, the practice times can be at such odd hours that the game can really disrupt the family schedule. One local high-school team practices at 4:00 A.M. daily. Keeping that kind of schedule could mess up my whole day.

5. *Injuries.* Hockey is a fast, rough game, and it has the expected number of injuries. Since the athletes move on skates, they are very sus-

ceptible to twists and sprains. Before your son competes, make sure you have good insurance coverage.

Individual Sports

Wrestling

1. *Opportunities.* Next to basketball, wrestling is becoming the second most popular winter sport in school and college athletic programs. In recent years, several high schools have added it to their programs, and the sport has picked up both participants and loyal fans. In addition, park districts and other organizations have created some programs for boys beginning as early as eight or nine years of age. Although there have been a few girls who have tried to compete, wrestling is still a male dominated sport. Since wrestling utilizes people of all sizes, and since it provides an atmosphere of open competition, it does offer a good alternative to basketball.

2. *Physical characteristics.* Since wrestling pairs the competition by weight, it is one of the few sports that offers an equal opportunity to every boy regardless of his size or shape. There are several theories about weight control. If your son decides to participate in any kind of organized wrestling program, I encourage you to take him first to a doctor or a health center that can measure his excess body fat either by submersion into water or by calipers. Based on this information, determine how much, if any, weight your son needs to lose. Then hold your ground. Don't let him go on any diets or weight restriction programs that would take him below his desired body fat weight.

The athlete needs to be strong for his size and to have some quickness. However, since raw natural speed is of no great asset, some of the quickness can be developed. Any boy who wants to work at becoming a good wrestler can develop a good measure of the physical characteristics required. So if your son has inherited the possibility of being small or not very fast, you may want to help him consider wrestling as a good sport for him.

3. *Mental characteristics.* Although there is a bit of a team flavor in school wrestling programs, during the match itself the athlete is entirely on his own. He is in the middle of the world, alone to accept his own joys and suffer his own frustrations and embarrassment.

The wrestler needs a ton of determination. A good wrestling match is almost a constant struggle against the maximum of the athlete's strength. If he relaxes for even an instant, he could lose the match in that moment. There is probably no other sport that demands such constant determination and strong will to survive.

4. *Costs.* Other than gym time, wrestling is a relatively inexpensive sport. There isn't much equipment, and that doesn't cost very much. Wrestling is also a portable sport because it doesn't require a very big area or an elaborate apparatus. The athlete can practice his moves almost anywhere. Parents of young wrestlers tell me that the athlete's own bed seems to be a favorite practice arena, particularly if he has younger brothers.

5. *Injuries.* Wrestling is a strenuous sport demanding constant muscle tension; consequently, there is always the possibility of strains and pulls. Wrestling rules attempt to protect the athlete against broken bones, but there are still a few of those.

Track

1. *Opportunities.* Although there are some nonschool youth programs in track and field, you have to hunt to find them. This is unfortunate because track is an excellent sport for boys and girls of all ages. It can utilize many people, is diverse enough to recognize different kinds of physical ability, and is inexpensive. If you have a child who is not particularly wild about one of the other sports opportunities available, you may want to contact your nearest Amateur Athletic Union (AAU) office to see what is available in track, or you may want to encourage those people to help you get something going in your area.

Some elementary schools do have programs such as annual play days where several schools get together and match children in races. Although there isn't much coaching, practice, or preparation, this is better than nothing. But school programs don't usually get into full swing until junior high school. Junior-high and high-school programs are available to almost everyone who wants to participate. If your school doesn't have a program for your son or daughter, go to the school personnel and suggest one. You may find them quite accepting of the idea. After all, this is a good sport, which can be inserted into an athletic program quite easily.

Track is also one of the most popular sports for adults. The athlete doesn't have to quit when he reaches a certain age, but just moves into another class and keeps running.

2. *Physical characteristics.* Good track athletes begin with a large

measure of natural ability. Speed is the most obvious of those natural assets. And speed is one of those abilities the athlete needs to bring from home. We coaches have never found a very effective way of turning a slow child into a fast one. Good coaches know how to teach people how to use their speed in such maneuvers as starting and pacing, but the athlete needs to provide the speed.

Track has enough different events that athletes with other abilities can find some spot. High jumpers can excel with good spring and coordination; pole vaulters need coordination and strength; hurdlers can compete with long and even strides; long distance runners utilize the natural ability of endurance; and shot putters and discus throwers need strength and coordination.

3. *Mental characteristics*. Track is similar to all other individual sports in that the athlete is alone in an event. There are no teammates to blame or rely on. Because of that, track is a good sport for people who are capable of accepting responsibility for their own performance. It is also a good sport for teaching that, too.

Track is also a sport that asks the athlete to accept himself as an opponent. Of course, there will be other people in the race to beat; but since a performance can be measured exactly, individual progress and goals are set according to that.

4. *Costs*. Unless your child is a hurdler or a pole vaulter, track can be a very inexpensive and portable sport. Runners, jumpers, and throwers can usually practice their events almost anywhere. Since shoes are the main cost, I recommend that if your child is beginning a career in track, you check with a shoe expert and get the athlete fitted with the right shoes. Running in the wrong shoes can burn out a budding track star more quickly than heat and humidity.

5. *Injuries*. Nothing is totally safe, and there have been a few unfortunate, serious accidents in track. If your child participates, talk about some of these dangers such as standing too close to the shot put circle or playing around with a pole when the child doesn't know how to use it. But other than that, track is the sport of muscle pulls and tears. If your child is a runner or a jumper, get somebody to teach proper methods of stretching and warming up. This is not absolute insurance, but it does minimize the possibility of injury.

Swimming

1. *Opportunities*. Organized competitive swimming is a great sport

because it utilizes several people and it offers almost identical opportunities to boys and girls. But it is limited by pool facilities. If you have a child who wants to swim competitively, go to your nearest swimming pool and check in. The pool coaches will be able to tell you everything you need to know about the opportunities available. If you don't know where the nearest pool is, call the park district or the nearest YMCA or YWCA.

Most state-school athletic associations now have organized and supervised school competition. But, of course, individual schools can participate only if they have pool facilities available. The odds are that your child won't have an opportunity to participate in a school program unless you make an effort to get the child to the pool.

2. *Physical characteristics.* Competitive swimmers are strong. In fact, weight lifting is a definite part of the training program for many swimmers. But unlike the football players who are trying to build bulk through weights, swimmers are trying to reduce the body bulk and increase the strength. Good swimmers also have strong hands and wrists.

3. *Mental characteristics.* Swimmers are much like track athletes but perhaps even more lonely. Since swimming is not the most popular spectator sport in the world, swimmers also go through the further challenge of being unknown athletes.

4. *Costs.* Unless you live in an area that is rich enough to provide pool facilities for its citizens, you will have to spend some money to support your swimmer. It costs to join those clubs or to buy pool time. On the other hand, a little swimsuit doesn't cost all that much, and you don't have to worry about fancy shoes.

5. *Injuries.* Although there are a few serious injuries, particularly in diving, swimming injuries are usually limited to muscle pulls and strains and eye and ear infections.

Gymnastics

1. *Opportunities.* Although gymnastics is not a sport for everybody, it is a good sport that can utilize a lot of athletes, offers equal opportunity to boys and girls, and can be started quite young. But again, the opportunities are limited simply because the sport requires elaborate facilities and equipment. So if you think gymnastics is the right sport for your child, you may need to find a private gymnastics club, clinic, or school. Once you contact those people, they can tell you what opportunities are available.

Most state-school athletic associations do sponsor gymnastics competition, but again it is limited to schools that have enough interest and money to provide the facilities for training and meets. If your child is a gymnast, you may or may not have a school program available to you.

2. *Physical characteristics.* Gymnastics requires the raw ingredients of flexibility and agility. From that, the athlete needs to develop strength in relationship to body bulk. The heavier the child is, the stronger he or she has to be until eventually some people get too big to develop the strength required to perform some of the moves.

3. *Mental characteristics.* As a sport, gymnastics requires some unusual mental outlooks. A gymnast has to be a daring person—not afraid of heights or of falling. Confidence and the courage to take risks are two more important requirements.

A good gymnast must also possess some aesthetic taste. A gymnastic routine must be performed with expertise and style—the gymnast must create physical pictures with the human body.

4. *Costs.* This is an expensive sport. Somebody has to pay for the gym time. Somebody has to pay for all that equipment. If your child is a gymnast, you will probably have to bear some of that cost.

5. *Injuries.* I am amazed that there aren't a lot of serious injuries in this sport with all the risk taking, but apparently the coaches and the athletes themselves know how to take care of themselves. Before you let your child participate, make sure to select an expert who can give good, solid coaching. The minor injuries include pulls, tears, strains, an occasional broken bone, hand blisters, and, most common among the younger athletes, skin tears in the palms.

Golf

1. *Opportunities.* Golf is popular among adults, but it may be one of the most limited individual sports for young people. Small children simply can't play. The game requires strength and coordination that come with size and age. It is also too expensive for many young people. But if you belong to a club or you enroll your child in a club, there are tournaments for young people beginning in the early teens. Again, most state-school athletic associations supervise golf competition, but the number of schools that participate is limited to ones with access to courses for practice.

This actually may be an unfortunate situation. Since golf is a sport that can be enjoyed by men and women of any age, perhaps young people could develop an interest earlier if there were more opportunities available.

2. *Physical characteristics.* A good golfer has good enough body control to make it perform accurately. In other words, coordination is important. It also helps to have strong hands and wrists and good hand and eye coordination. Golf gives no edge to size, speed, or even overall strength. This makes it a good alternative for the young person who may not have the natural athletic abilities to excel in some of the other sports.

3. *Mental characteristics.* A good golfer needs to be able to concentrate completely and to have confidence. Actually, the sport not only requires concentration and confidence but it also teaches these traits.

4. *Costs.* This is an expensive game. Even after one has paid the greens fees either through membership or on a day-by-day basis, one still has to buy shoes, clubs, bags, and balls (if he is like me, lots and lots of balls).

5. *Injuries.* If the athlete is careful and doesn't get hit by a club, there aren't too many things that can cause injuries on the golf course other than lightning and snake bites.

Tennis

1. *Opportunities.* Tennis is not a sport for toddlers, but boys and girls can pick it fairly early and stay with the game through retirement. School programs are sometimes limited because some schools don't have the facilities, but there are enough park districts, private clubs, and specially sponsored programs to provide almost every person with an opportunity to play somewhere. Even if a child doesn't play in an organized program, tennis is a good game for informal matches and family-scheduled games.

2. *Physical characteristics.* There is some advantage to speed, but the most important natural ability is quickness—the ability to move three or four feet instantly and instinctively. The tennis player also needs to have strong hands and wrists and to be in good enough physical condition to endure the whole match. The short, explosive moves of tennis demand more physical conditioning than some other sports where the movement is for more extended periods of time.

3. *Mental characteristics.* Tennis is a finesse game that demands concentration and savvy. The good player must anticipate and move into position even before the opponent hits the ball. Since tennis is a game

against a real opponent, the good player has to have some competitive determination.

4. *Costs.* If courts are available, tennis is only moderately expensive. Good racquets will cost from fifty dollars up and balls do wear out. But if you have to rent court space or join a club, the expense could be as much as swimming.

5. *Injuries.* Tennis puts unusual emphasis and movement on some muscles and joints. Young players occasionally suffer some inflammation in the shoulder and elbow. Other than that, everybody is eligible for blisters and pulls; and in the summertime, heat exhaustion is always a possibility unless the young players have been taught how to avoid overexertion.

This concludes my analysis of some of the most common team and individual sports. I realize that by generalizing the information, I have taken several risks. I might not have given you enough details; I might have given some information that isn't accurate for a specific location or with a specific athlete; or I might have left out your favorite sport. If any of those things happened to you, I apologize, but I urge you to consider my overall purpose in this chapter.

As your child enters the age when he or she may want to begin active participation in athletics, explore with your child all the possibilities available before making a final decision. Some children are good enough athletes to excel in most sports, and they can choose one or many and do well. But the others do need to make some decision, and it is sad to see a person who for one reason or another has tried to achieve some distinction in the wrong sport. A few years ago, a talented, well-built athlete came to our college to play basketball. Despite the fact that his size was in bulk rather than height, he was a fair college basketball player. His senior year, he decided to try football. During that year, he demonstrated enough skill to indicate that he could have been a great small-college football player, but he had specialized all those other years in the other sport.

Before your child makes a decision, make sure all the opportunities available have been explored. Once that has been done, you will need to help with making some choices, and that is the subject of the next chapter.

What Parents Ask

1. *Everytime I turn around, our high school adds some new sport to its program. Why do we need anything more than the good old football, basketball, and baseball?*

If there is anything positive to be learned from sports, and I believe there is, every child should have an opportunity to learn those lessons. Some children are too little for football or too slow for basketball, but a variety of sports will provide every child with an opportunity to do something regardless of body type.

2. *How soon does a child have to decide on a specific sport?*

That depends on the child's interests, abilities, commitment to sports, and expectations. Some children want to sample several sports, but some want to focus their interest on one.

3. *I don't mind if my child plays sports, but I don't want him to get hurt. What is the safest sport available?*

Take your pick. I could quote statistics, but they wouldn't help much because statistics don't always tell the whole story. If I picked a sport for you, your child would probably fall and break an arm walking to practice. I have coached entire football seasons without a single time-loss injury. I have coached track seasons where half the runners were out for some reason. We never know. From what I have seen in gyms and on fields in recent years, cheerleading looks to be about the most dangerous activity going on.

14. *Choosing the Game*

Every time I remember Max, I am reminded that in spite of our best efforts people sometimes still turn out all right. I first met Max when he was forced by school and state policy to take my freshman P.E. program. By then, Max was about on his last leg, to use an athletic cliché.

He was the third son of an active family. His father was an avid summer league softball player, and his mother was good enough in tennis and racquetball to enter some local tournaments. The older brothers were semi-stars in youth football and baseball, and the father even got involved in coaching.

But then there was Max. Max just didn't have good hand and eye coordination, and he didn't have quick feet. Now in this case, and thousands of others like it, it is hard to tell which came first, failure or lack of interest in sports, but Max was plagued with both. He simply wasn't very good, and he just didn't want to make the effort to get any better. He preferred sitting home and watching television.

But the problem was deeper than sports. He wasn't too hot in the classroom either. He seemed to be smart enough, but he didn't push himself to make the grades. By the time he became a freshman, that combination of no interest in sports and below-average academic work had locked him into friendships with some other students who, in the same shape as he, weren't going to encourage him very much. It was a group that seemed to be making the most out of its lack of success. And this kind of group is always a bit questionable. What might they try to achieve self-identity and recognition?

That whole gang enrolled in my second-hour freshman P.E. class. Of course, the class was bigger than that small group, but their apathy was pervasive enough to set a lackluster tone for the whole class. I didn't care all that much as long as they tried hard enough to look busy and sweat a bit. But one day, they all got out of hand at the same time. Right at the beginning of the class, they started griping about what activity we had for that day. They didn't want to play. It wasn't fun. It was too hot. And finally, the zinger, it was boring. I was reasonable for a moment, but then I lost my temper.

One word of caution. Whatever you do, never make an old coach angry. Since we are used to making snap, cool decisions in the heat of battle, we welcome an opportunity to fly off the handle. When I get angry, I get angry. I look mad and bellow loud—loud enough that I usually get my way.

This time it was an order with a threat. "If you don't want to do what I offer you, then you just run laps around the track until I tell you to stop. Get out there and get started!"

I don't know whether I scared Max or whether he was just looking for an opportunity, but he started running, really running, and he kept it up. At first, I really didn't notice, but after a few laps, I saw that he was passing everyone about once every two laps. He ran that way the whole period.

Always on the lookout for an athlete, I took my observation to the cross-country coach. He was skeptical, but since he didn't have many athletes, he decided to take a chance and talk to Max. Max accepted the offer and agreed to try cross-country. Within two weeks, Max was the fastest freshman on the team. By the end of the season, he was the fastest freshman in the conference. As a sophomore, he was the fastest cross-country runner in school. As a senior, he was the fastest in the state. He is now running cross-country at a small college where he is majoring in psychology.

But more than that success, Max became a successful and popular high-school student. When he joined the cross-country team, he entered a new social group. He began to work harder in his classes and attracted attention with his cheerfulness. Like many young persons, Max experienced success in one area of his life that produced success in the other areas. Nothing begets winning like winning.

I want you to remember Max. Max represents a thousand and maybe a million other kids who flounder around in life because, for some reason, they simply have not discovered the right sport.

I don't want to throw you into a state of panic, but I do want to make the point that your child's decision about which sport or sports to pursue can be a very important decision. It deserves some attention.

Whose Decision?

The first question you as a concerned parent must ask is, whose decision is this in the first place? Who has the responsibility of making that potentially important decision about which sport or sports?

Be careful. The right answer may not be the easiest one to carry out. We all love our children and our image of ourselves as loving parents enough that we want to scream out our answer to that preposterous question, "Well, it's the child's decision, of course. I wouldn't dare impose my will about such a thing on my child." But don't bet on that. We adults frequently impose our wills on children and make decisions for them without our ever realizing it.

Some children begin so young in organized sports that they have no idea how to make a decision, much less decide whether they like the activity or not. In our town, we now have organized soccer for six-year-olds. I can't believe that those six-year-olds have exercised their right of choice and have employed all the decision-making techniques in electing to participate. They are in soccer because their parents made that decision for them. Of course, some of them, probably most of them, are having a good time and are making the activity valuable; but the parents still made the decision for them.

I am not criticizing that approach. I just want to make the point that if your child begins to participate in organized sports at a young age, you will need to be very sensitive to that child's reactions. In the opening illustration, Max began sports early and participated in a rather wide range, but he had never really made the decision himself. As he grew older, his lack of ability in the sports that his parents chose for him caused him some problems. Fortunately, he overcame those problems when he finally reached the point where he made his own choice.

Parents impose their wills on children in subtle ways. All parents have expectations for their children. We want them to achieve certain goals and perform at certain levels of ability. But sometimes those expectations have a way of becoming serious challenges and even dares for the children to perform. When that happens, they find themselves participating in a sport because their parents expect them to. If that is the case, they will never give the sport their maximum talent or interest. They will feel as if they are carrying their parents on their backs as they try to participate.

Let me tell you about my college friend, Joe. Joe's father had been a Major League baseball player, so Joe naturally started organized baseball as soon as he was old enough and strong enough to beat mud out of his cleats with a bat.

Joe excelled. All through youth programs and high school, he was always the best, always on the all-star team. He filled his room with trophies and his dad with pride. Scouts came. College coaches came. Everybody agreed that he had a great future. But when Joe started college he didn't even go out for baseball. He quit the sport entirely and concentrated on football.

When people asked him why, his answer was rather flimsy. "I just don't like baseball anymore." Why had this sport at which he was so excellent suddenly lost its appeal? Could it be that he felt too much silent pressure to succeed, that he couldn't carry the load and so chose his own sport instead of his father's?

The premise in this book is that sports and athletes are mutually beneficial to each other. If a young athlete has chosen an activity, that athlete will most likely make a stronger commitment to it, will contribute more to the sport, and get more out of participation. On the other hand, if that young athlete feels pressured into the activity, there will never be the kind of full commitment that promotes integrity, discipline, and growth. There may be excellence and trophies, but the experience could have been much more positive if the athlete had been given the right to choose.

"But," you reply, "some kids simply don't know what's good for them. I can make a better evaluation of the situation and I have the child's best interest at heart." I answer that with an illustration not from sports but from the orchestra. When Chuck started fifth grade and decided to join the orchestra, he was the biggest boy in the class. The teacher, a solid, conscientious orchestra director, looked at Chuck's size and assigned him to the bass violin. He was the only person in class big enough to handle it. But Chuck wanted to play the cello. He liked the music it made. But what does a fifth-grader know about his own likes and dislikes? Chuck played the bass violin as he had been told—but he never did well. Finally, when he reached seventh grade, he announced to his parents, the orchestra director, and the world that he was now old enough to quit orchestra because he didn't like it anymore. But in the ensuing discussion, which almost always follows such announcements from our children or our participants, Chuck admitted that he preferred the cello.

He was granted a reprieve and was permitted to change instruments. He practiced hard, became quite good, and continued to play the cello throughout high school. He still plays it as a hobby.

Let me summarize this. Regardless of age, your child is old enough to know what he or she enjoys. Since the purpose of sports participation is to have a good time, you need to make sure your child is given the right to make the decision to participate.

Factors in the Sports Decision

Does this mean that you sit calmly while your child makes such an important decision? Of course not. This is an important time, and your young athlete needs your help. Let's look at some of the factors that go into making this decision, and talk about how you can help your child assess those factors.

1. Interest

The experts—child psychologists and educators—argue loud and long over the elusive but powerful characteristic of interest. Why are individuals interested in the things that interest them? Why do some middle-aged people run marathons and others balk at running across the street? Why do some people watch baseball everyday, but wouldn't watch a football game on the threat of torture? After twenty-five years in teaching and coaching, I am convinced that interest is learned, at least in part, and is not just a feeling unique to this individual. In other words, if your child is interested in soccer, wrestling, football, basketball, or TV programs, that interest was learned somewhere.

"So then," you ask quickly, "what can I do to make sure my child learns an interest in the sport I would like for him to play?" Although I can't guarantee the results, I can make some suggestions. The first lesson is exposure. We don't usually become excited about something we know absolutely nothing about. If you want to end up with a strong commitment based on interest, you need to expose your child to enough sports to have something to choose from. In the interest of your child's sports decision, you may find yourself in some places which don't seem too exciting to you. Just remember that you are there because of your child. Let me say this emphatically. If you are interested in your child's sports decision, make sure you at least introduce every sport available in your community.

A second factor that builds interest is success. Most of us like to do what we do well. Your child needs to have some success in order to develop a healthy interest in any activity. Since I will discuss some of the reasons for success later, let me just say here that sports success is a rather demanding ideal. In sports, being average is usually not good enough. Most of us envision ourselves as stars or winners. When I was a child playing backyard baseball, I never fantasized about being some dud with a .235 batting average. I was always the hero, the star. You need to remember that when your child starts into a sport. There may be some strong demands to succeed. However, if a child learns how to manage those expectations, and learns to enjoy the activity, that child will probably develop enough interest to work hard and achieve some measure of success.

As a football coach, I see this every fall. Some promising young athlete enters our program as a freshman, but he is too small and too slow to play. Through sheer determination and hard work produced by interest, he develops quickness and strength and becomes a valuable member of the team by the time he is a junior. Those stories are too common to ignore the power of interest in athletic success.

2. Growth Expectations

The process of creation is wonderful and mysterious. When we think we have it figured out scientifically, we run into all sorts of exceptions. Thus, we can never guarantee accuracy in our predictions about how our children will look after they are grown. We can often make educated guesses, though, and experts have designed some elaborate charts and formulas for determining growth potential of children. One of the best and simplest indicators is still the factor of heritage. Presently, I have a football player on my team who is six feet five and 260 pounds. I am not really surprised. His father is six feet three and his mother is six feet one. Since you know your child's parents, grandparents, uncles, and aunts, you may want to discuss together what can be expected in terms of ultimate size and body type.

Unfortunately, the time schedule of growth is another matter, strictly between God and the child. Some children grow and mature physically when they are very young. Some have growth and body maturity spurts as young adolescents or about the time of puberty. Some people experience that growth spurt in their early twenties.

This is, without a doubt, the toughest factor in this process of picking a sport. Although we may be certain that a particular child will have the height to be a basketball player eventually, we don't know whether that height will come soon enough for the child to enjoy some success in the sport before too many setbacks are encountered. Let me illustrate.

Randall was the tallest boy on the sixth-grade basketball team and was a starter. By the eighth grade, he still had above average height, but his coordination had not caught up with his growth pattern. At this point, the coaches moved him to the "B" team. He didn't quit, his parents didn't raise a fuss, and he maintained a strong interest in basketball. He kept practicing and going to camps. Eventually he made the high-school basketball team and was a starter in his senior year. The important thing was that he was able to work through his growth patterns and skill levels to the point of being able to participate in a sport in which he had a high interest.

On the other hand, Brent was never able to survive the cut system of school basketball programs. From seventh grade to tenth grade, he went out every year but was among the first to be released. Finally, he quit trying for the school team but kept his interest active in a church league. As a high-school senior, he had reached six feet four and had developed coordination; he became an excellent basketball player and destroyed all church league competition.

Matt had the same circumstances. He and his folks knew he would someday grow tall. They just never knew when. But the frustration of getting cut every year while he was waiting for that spurt finally destroyed his confidence, and in his senior year, he was the tallest spectator in the stands.

The stories of the early growers are about as sad as those of the late growers. The child whose growth pattern is a little ahead of schedule could develop an unfortunate attitude about his own ability. If he is bigger than his peers, he will have some early success; but when his peers catch up, he could spend a lot of time brooding over where the success went. Frequently, bigger children perform on size and maturity rather than on skill development, technique, or even effort; so when their peers catch up and they don't have the size advantage anymore, they are left behind.

Roy was the strongest, most physically mature boy in his class. As a five-foot-eight eighth grader, he excelled in football and basketball. In football, he was a natural fullback, and he was the center in basketball. He worked hard to develop skills and techniques of playing center. He became quite good at it, too. As a senior, Roy was still five eight. He was no longer the tallest, the strongest, or the fastest. He did make the adjustment in football and became an excellent defensive lineman, but there is little call for a high-school basketball center of his size. Roy had learned the wrong set of skills when he was bigger than everyone else, and he never made the adjustment as his peers caught up.

Since you have no control over the time schedule of those growth patterns, you and your child will have to learn to accept and adjust to those changing bodies and circumstances in order for you to determine how much success and happiness your child may get from a particular activity.

3. Environmental Conditions

Sometimes an athlete's physical environment dictates the choice of activities. In Mark's case, this was true. He came from a small rural community in central Indiana where the school he attended had only basketball and baseball. In his sophomore year, however, his school was consolidated with a larger school. Now he had several options. His parents were strong advocates of Mark's playing basketball, but they were very hesitant about his participation in football. Since he had been an early maturer in his basketball skills, his coach felt he had greater potential in football, and he spent a great amount of time talking to Mark's parents trying to convince them of this. They would have to make a number of sacrifices in order for him to participate in football since it was a preschool sport for practice. This would take time away from working on the farm. It meant many trips back and forth from home, which was seventeen miles one way, and many late dinners.

Mark's parents were supportive of his athletic choice and said that he could play football. He started on the first string as a sophomore and junior, and was a first team all-stater as a senior, earning a four-year scholarship to the state university. He was a three-year starter as a defensive back and at the conclusion of his senior year, he was chosen to play in the Hula Bowl in Hawaii. Mark also played basketball but not with the same success, and he starred in track as well. I think this was accomplished because of his parents' openness and willingness to play a supportive role while letting their son make his choices.

4. Mental Attitude

As discussed earlier, some sports require a certain mindset if the athlete is to be happy or successful. Since you are the one person in the world who knows your child best, you are the only person around who can help assess your child's personality or mental attitude in regard to a sports decision. That statement assumes that you are mature enough to help your child explore all the possibilities, and assumes that you are able to make an honest evaluation of your child's personality.

Don't be deceived. He may be big, but he may not have the mental aggressiveness it takes to enjoy football. She may be tall, but she may not enjoy the rapid pace of basketball. You have lived with your child long enough to learn such things. Use that knowledge to help your child make the decision.

For example, if your child enjoys being alone or doesn't accept criticism very well, it is probably not wise to think about being in a team sport. That kind of personality is not a human flaw. It isn't something your child should be ashamed of. It is simply an important factor that should be weighed in choosing a sport.

What if that particular child who happens to like being alone wants to play a team sport such as baseball? I wouldn't discourage that decision, but I would listen to what such a desire means to the child. Perhaps a strong self-image is lacking, and your child sees success in the popular sport as a cure for that. If that is the case, and success is not an early result of choosing that sport, the subsequent pain could be severe and even damaging.

That time when your child is beginning to be active in sports participation is a very special time. Although the decision may not rank up there with choosing a spouse or selecting a college, it is still a significant decision in the process of growing. You will want to be very close to your child during this time. You will need to watch for subtle changes in mood or expressions of anger or happiness. You will want to make sure your child is confident enough to come and talk with you at any time. You will want to check the progress in other areas because sports participation is not just an isolated event. It has a ripple effect in everything the child does.

How Many Sports?

Before we answer this question, let's develop a three-point system for categorizing the degrees of participation: casual, experimental, and full.

Unless your child is glued to the TV or is a thoroughgoing bookworm, he or she will play casual games, and this is good; the more the better. Help him. Even if he is a football player, put a hoop up. If she is a baseball player, buy her a soccer ball. If he is a basketball player, take him swimming. This is healthy play and is a part of being a child. Don't worry if he is not very good as long as he is enjoying it. Don't worry if she doesn't know the rules or the finer points as well as you would like. Don't pressure child's play into organized and disciplined routine.

From this casual relationship, your child may want to experiment with several sports or may want to play whatever is in season. Again, this is healthy if the family and study habits can stand that much intensity for that long a time. But you and the child need to keep in mind that this is really experimenting. You should make it clear by both your attitude and your words that a choice can be made to concentrate whenever it seems right to the child.

From this experimentation, almost every athlete eventually makes a choice of full commitment to a single sport. This is always a significant choice regardless of when it is made. Very active children, physically mature children, or gifted athletes may delay that decision for awhile, but the average athlete will find more success in sports if a choice can be made regarding an area of concentration fairly early. That extra time for practice and study of the sport is usually needed.

I recently asked Tony Hampton, a former U.S. team gymnast and presently a gym instructor and coach, "What would you have done if you had never discovered your ability in gymnastics?" His answer was so fascinating and so instructive that I offer it in its total form.

When I was first asked to write about what I would have done if I had not spent more than half of my life doing gymnastics, I thought the answer would be easy. Boy! Was I wrong.

This is a question I often thought about, but I never examined it in much detail. I would just answer it by saying, "I would probably be in some other sport," and that was that.

The best way to answer the question, "what would I be doing if I were not in gymnastics?" is to start out by explaining why I chose gymnastics and the path that I did take. I started gymnastics when I was thirteen and in the midst of two other sports that I was having a certain amount of success in. I had two starting positions in football, and in track I was doing the long jump and pole vault. Some of my friends went out for gymnastics so I decided to go along with the crowd and tried out also. Even though I was doing well in the other two sports, they began to fall by the wayside. When it got tough in football or in track, my first instinct was to quit, and after awhile that is what happened. I guess I did not care enough to try a little harder until the rough spots smoothed out. In gymnastics, it was a different story; when it got tough, there was always a driving force inside of me that made me want to go back and overcome any problems that I had and do better. That driving force that is inside of me is unexplainable, but it is there even today. I always knew that if I tried a little harder I could accomplish what I wanted to do.

The drive I have for gymnastics led me to many championships. It led me to an athletic scholarship and a fine college career. I have also learned to use that force in other aspects in my life but not to its full potential like in gymnastics. I am sure that in time I will learn to use it to its full extent.

In conclusion, I could only come up with one answer. The driving force and the energy that I had for gymnastics would never have surfaced. I feel it would have stayed locked away somewhere in my brain. Sure, I would have probably done another sport, but I am also sure that I would not have had the degree of success that I had in gymnastics. I feel extremely lucky that I did discover my driving force and was able to use it in its full potential. A number of people never find their driving force and never find what they do best, so they have to settle for something less.

I could go on in more detail about my conclusion, but I know that whatever course I might have taken in my life, I would not be as happy as I am now.

As you can see, the decision your child has to make about a sport can be significant. It deserves your attention, study, and honesty.

Now, let's look at some of the opportunities and programs available to your young athlete, regardless of the sport chosen.

What Parents Ask

1. *My daughter wants to quit basketball. Should I let her?*

   That question is deserved. All through this book, you've been told that sports should be fun and that the athlete should make the decisions. But what about quitting? Is that different? Maybe! The reason your daughter wants to quit is the deciding factor. Is she too lazy to work? Does she like the coach? Is she frustrated or does she just want to goof off? If she is quitting for any of those reasons, we urge you to urge her not to quit in order to run away from a situation that can be corrected. Is she tired or burned out? If so, you may want to propose a resting period for her—a recess rather than a termination. Does she hate the sport or is she so bad at it that she is being humiliated? If so, hear her, please! Make sure you help her explore the reasons so she can feel confident about the ultimate decision.

2. *My son plays four different sports. Is that too many?*

   Only you and he can answer that question, but first ask some other questions. Is he happy? Is he well-balanced? Does he keep his school studies up? Does he have friends? Does he want to spend all his time playing sports?

3. *I have tried to introduce my son to several sports. I have taken him out to play basketball, baseball, football, and tennis, and he acts completely uninterested in learning or even trying to learn those sports. But I catch him in the backyard playing ball with his friends. What is going on?*

   Probably he perceives that you are trying to force him into a deeper relationship with the sport than he wants. This may not be true, but if he perceives it, it is truth for him. You may be rushing him. Back off a bit and see if his interest develops through the years.

15. *Little Leagues and Other Parent Programs*

For the purpose of simplification, the youth sports opportunities have been divided into three classes: parent programs, school programs, and club or clinic programs. For no particular reason, the discussion will begin with parent programs.

Although some organizations and some supporters may take offense to gathering all parent organization opportunities under one umbrella, this distinction is still possible. There is a wide variety of organizational structures, ranging all the way from loosely structured programs of local park districts to highly developed organizations with specific rules and national playoff opportunities. But for the athlete, for that youngster who is the cause and the backbone of the program in the first place, parent-run baseball is parent-run baseball whether it is a highly structured and widely known Little League or a local organization. The programs may be different for the coaches, officials, and administrators, but the programs still provide similar opportunities for the players.

Perhaps the one thing I need to keep clear is that although the term *Little League* has come to mean any kind of nonschool youth sports program, the name actually refers to a nationwide organization and should always be capitalized. This in itself is an interesting compliment, attesting to the success of the Little League organization. Just as we call jeans Levi's, soda Coke, and tissues Kleenex, we have a tendency to call all youth baseball Little League.

A Matter of Leadership

When this chapter on parent programs—whether Little League or not—was originally planned, we thought we would list advantages and disadvantages of your child's participation in parent-run sports programs. But after lengthy investigation, it became clear that the advantages and the disadvantages grow out of the same characteristics. The difference is a matter of leadership.

Whether any one characteristic of the program will make a positive and significant contribution to your child's athletic, emotional, and mental growth depends on the kind of leadership the program has. If coaches and parents are overzealous or on ego-trips and lose sight of the objectives of the program, your child will have to struggle to get anything good out of participation and, in fact, could learn a lot of bad skills and attitudes. On the other hand, if the coaches and parents are sincerely interested in helping young people have fun, your child could get a world of good from the program.

To emphasize this point more fully, an expert was consulted. Jack Richard has devoted more than thirty years to the development of youth baseball for boys and softball for girls in a small southern Indiana town. He started this program in 1950. I have seen hundreds of young boys and girls go through the program and enjoy a strongly structured activity that provides them with the basic fundamental aspects of the game. I have seen a community come together to support their program by providing proper equipment and excellent facilities. Many donated hours have been directed toward the development of this program where the primary objective was to meet the needs of the youngsters.

Here is what Jack says about his experiences:

There are those who get involved in these youth programs just as long as their sons or daughters are eligible. There are some who get into them through clubs and civic organizations. There are a few who do it because they actually enjoy helping the young and inexperienced. Some find it an enjoyable way to spend their spare hours no matter how they were drawn into the programs.

One of the most glaring weaknesses of parental participation is that some are in it only for the sake of promoting their own son's or daughter's capabilities. They see these programs as opportunities to show how much better their offspring can perform versus others. Theirs become the pitchers or quarterbacks even though they aren't the best for the position.

The best operated programs are the ones where the leadership is continuous. I once heard a top administrator of one of these programs say, "Don't pay much attention to the loud-mouthed critics because they won't last. Your real help will come from the softer speaking people who roll up their sleeves and pitch in." However, since most of the help is parental oriented, it is therefore usually temporary. Continuity is sometimes provided due to large families with several sons and/or daughters going through the same program. Good leadership will call on the better ones to come back while allowing the wrong type to fade away.

Another point which should be made is that these programs are like government. You should not complain of the type of leadership if you aren't willing to help yourself. It is a privilege like voting. Go to the polls. Go to the meetings. Go to the games. Lend a hand—not just a mouth. Do not just take from the program. Give something. A participant is usually better informed than the audience. The coach is closer to the game than a fan. The concession worker is better prepared than the screaming mother. A board member can do more than the umpire critic to pave the way for a growing child.

Now that we have established the importance of leadership, let's take a look at some of those other characteristics that can be turned into pleasant experiences or traumatic nightmares for your child, depending on how they are handled.

Opportunity

These programs provide millions of children with organized sports opportunity. In spite of all the criticism, in spite of all the warnings of dangers, in spite of all the things that can go right or wrong, parent-run sports programs provide the greatest opportunity, and in many cases the only opportunity, for children to participate in organized sports. Most of the time this opportunity is open to any child who wants to participate regardless of athletic talent or growth, and in many of these programs, league rules stipulate that all players actually get into the contest for some portion of the game. Since there are parent-run programs in almost every town or park district in the nation, nearly every child has some opportunity to participate.

There are simply no other programs providing this kind of opportunity for children. If you and your child have decided that he or she should get involved in organized sports before the age when school sports begin to form, you probably have no choice but to put him or her into a parent-run program of some kind.

These programs are usually inexpensive enough to be available to most children regardless of family finances. Although some ask from each player a small fee, most of them pay for expenses—uniforms, equipment, upkeep and official pay—with money donated from civic-minded people and businesses or earned from selling drives.

The problem with this open participation opportunity is that these programs attract the extremes of ability and put them on the same teams and in direct competition. For example, some programs base their team divisions on three-year age groups. This just permits too much diversity. When a child is that young, every year makes a big difference in size, development, and maturity. There is a huge gap between most ten-year-olds and twelve-year-olds. These age brackets can cause those players on the bottom end some tough times. If your child is an average size and at the younger end of the team's age bracket, you will have to work hard to keep discouragement down. You will have to practice skills with your child because the older players will be better by strength of experience.

Some programs, such as some park-district football, try to balance this grouping according to size. But in some situations, this may be even worse. A seventy-five-pound twelve-year-old is more mature than a seventy-five-pound nine-year-old, and thus simply has an advantage.

But despite these minor problems, these programs still provide opportunity. If your child wants to participate in sports, there is probably something available. To find those opportunities you can contact your child's school, your local park district, or the sports desk of a local newspaper. Somebody will know how to help you find the right team.

Family Events

These programs are family affairs and can be a great thing for a family. As the name suggests, parent-run programs bring parents into close contact with their children in all phases of sport activity. They also bring parents into a special knowledge and feel for the program. Of course, when the parents all agree cheerfully on all decisions about such matters as who should start, who should pitch, what position each player is best at, or game strategies, it is good to have parents this close to the activity. They are in a much better position to help their own children work on skills and develop proper attitudes toward the sport. They are more intense in their support and encouragement, and they are available for transportation, snacks, and other details.

On the other hand, when the parents don't agree, having all parents this close to the action can become a problem. In most parent-run programs, coaches simply don't enjoy the same kind of distance from parent interests as coaches in school programs do. Their decisions are frequently open to criticism, and they may have a greater tendency to bend to parent pressure. This can create chaos because not all players can pitch or play quarterback. If the program is to work smoothly, someone has to have enough freedom to make decisions. If not, the program then becomes a disorganized parents' club with children caught in the middle.

If your child's sports opportunity is limited to a program that has too much parent interference, do the child a favor. Either get him or her out before the program destroys all confidence and love for the game or, better yet, become part of the leadership and help those interfering parents calm down enough to give somebody the freedom to run a disciplined program.

The Serious Approach

Frequently, parent-run programs take themselves very seriously. These parents want to supply the very best for their children, regardless of age or ability. We have all seen the fancy uniforms, the nice park, the expensive equipment, the professional-looking referees or umpires, and the crucial game intensity. This is not really a bad thing in itself. I don't want to criticize parents for providing the best for their children when they can afford it. But fancy uniforms and fields communicate an important message to young players. This is a serious business. This is not the place to goof off or fool around or act childish. These are adult circumstances in an adult situation. The child is expected to treat the opportunity like an adult.

This attitude can put a lot of the wrong kind of pressure on young children, which can really be damaging in years to come. The first danger is that the situation can take the fun out of the sport for the players; and, as I have said before and often, if the game isn't fun, it isn't a game. This kind of intensity too early can burn out young players. Even the best of the young athletes can get so much glory at a young age that they can't handle the pressures of moving from youth programs to the next division where the equipment isn't as fine and the rewards aren't as great.

The one thing that you as a parent and perhaps as part of the leadership of a parent-run program need to keep in mind is that these sports programs were designed as a service to children. Any time a service begins to take itself too seriously, it ceases to be a service and becomes an obligation and a tyrant to the people it was designed to serve, in this case young athletes who need an opportunity to have fun with a sport.

Coaching

The coaching is not professional. In fact, most of the time, the coaches aren't even trained for their work. If handled correctly, this could be a definite advantage. There is nothing in the books that says that a person has to have a college degree in physical education or child psychology to understand sports and children. Some of the best coaches are those conscientious people who work another job every day and come out in the evening to help young people learn to love a sport.

At the same time, the worst coaches are those who simply don't understand sports, don't understand coaching, and surely don't understand children. In a later chapter, the importance of the coach will be discussed in depth. Here, I will just whet your appetite by saying that the coach is ultimately responsible for the attitude your child has for the game and maybe even for himself. In fact, I doubt that even most coaches understand the extent of their influence over the lives of the children who play for them.

If you are in a position to help your child make a choice about a program, search for the one with the most understanding coach. As far as your child is concerned, this is the difference between a good program and a bad one, between a positive experience, which provides a lifetime of happy memories, and a bad experience, which is suppressed as much as possible.

All coaches are capable of having the same strengths or weaknesses regardless of their training, but inexperienced coaches are more susceptible to those three problems noted above: they don't understand the sport, they don't understand coaching, or they don't understand children.

In each of these areas, television, or at least publicity, is one source of confusion. These games played by children are a different breed from these games played by monstrous athletes who have been in the sport for a quarter of a century. A good coach must spend some time thinking about the spirit and strategy of the game for the age group he is coaching. If a volunteer coach is exposed to too much pro or major college sports on television, he may get the idea that what he sees he should be doing with his nine-year-old. Unfortunately, the players are not big or wise enough or skillful enough to execute their assignments. He has given them demands they can't carry out.

Television also often overdramatizes superficial points. Professional football coverage would have us believe that intense ferocity is the crowning achievement of any good football player. This just isn't true. Football does not put any premium on ferocity. Some good players have been aggressive, but a football player must be calm and thoughtful. If any coach has gained his knowledge of the sport from any of these sources of inaccuracy, he will miss the main thrust of the sport when he tries to teach it to his players.

Some coaches, experienced and inexperienced, trained and untrained, don't understand coaching. The biggest difficulty here is understanding authority and how to use it. Any coach who hasn't thought about how to use authority doesn't understand coaching, and he can make one of two mistakes. Either he can be afraid of his authority and reap disorganization or he can be afraid of his authority and become an unbearable tyrant.

The coach who is afraid to take charge, make decisions, or discipline the team is a sad enough story, but the other extreme is tragic. Discipline is one thing. Verbal or physical abuse is another. We can't ever confuse the two. No coach has a right to abuse a player. That is a mandate.

Coaches need to understand children. My niece came home from her second day in first grade quite excited. The coach had come to the classroom to announce that the next day they would all go to the gym to play with basketballs and practice their stumbling. I am sure the coach said something else, but that isn't what my niece heard. He had used words the first-graders didn't understand. I hope he has a sense of humor.

The coach doesn't have to be a professional psychologist. He just needs to be sensitive, to use common sense, and to approach the sport with the same intensity the child brings.

A Good Time

The primary aims of parent-run programs are involvement and fun. If you let your child participate in a parent-run sports program, expect him or her to have a good time. If that isn't happening, you are missing your number one objective. You need to think about your child's experience.

By putting the emphasis on enjoyment, you accomplish two purposes. You help your child enjoy childhood without all the pressures of trying to win a world championship before the age of nine, and you don't put more expectations on the program than it can fulfill.

Through parent-run programs, your child may develop top body condition, may perfect all the skills to a professional level, may master all the minute strategies of each detail of the sport, may even become a world champion. And in the process you may win a million dollars in the lottery, too. But you may not. Don't put your expectations too high.

These programs are designed to provide opportunities to participate. They are not designed to find and train the next generation of major leaguers. If your child is a world class athlete, that talent will show up regardless of how early or late a start in the sport is made.

What should be the expected outcome of a youth program? When I moved to Illinois as a football coach, the first year we had two youth all-star teams that traveled to Boston to play in a championship. Many people questioned whether this was educationally sound. I think it was. It was an experience those children will never forget. For some, it will be their only opportunity to see some of the historical sites in our nation. They lived with other people in another geographic area.

Where did they go from there? The next year they went to different junior high schools, and two years later they went to the two different high schools in the community. Five moved away. Sixty-five percent played four years in high school. Three were all-staters. Four received college scholarships. Two others continued to play in college. I will let you draw your own conclusions.

If parent-run programs have the right kind of leadership and the right kind of coaches, they can provide an excellent service both to the community and to the youth of that community. Just don't expect them to do more than they are capable of.

What Parents Ask

1. *When will my son be old enough to start organized youth baseball?*

In many communities, there are programs for children as young as six years old. But no child is old enough to start playing games until he has played enough backyard ball to be able to catch, throw, swing a bat, and run the bases. If your son hasn't mastered those skills yet, he is too young to play organized baseball.

2. *I don't have time to teach him those things. Won't the organized ball help him learn?*

No! If you put a child in a game before he has learned the basic skills, he is going to get hurt, either physically or emotionally. If you don't have the time to play catch with your child, and you want him to learn how, hire somebody to do it for you. My number is in the book.

3. *My daughter would love to play softball, but the fathers who run the team are always fighting and arguing and doing things to spite each other. What should I do?*

Well, you can take her out or you can get involved yourself and try to ease the problems. Those are about your only two options. When parents begin to fuss with each other, they probably won't change much until their athletes leave the program.

16. *School Programs*

Now that we have looked at those parent-run programs, which are growing so rapidly in nearly every community throughout the nation, we need to look at the other stronghold of youth sports, the schools. Actually, having sports in schools is something of an American oddity. Although I am not sure I know when or how this all got started, the school, particularly the high school, is still the primary agent for providing sports opportunities for young athletes and their fans.

In this chapter, we will take a look at each level of school sports—elementary, junior high, high school, junior college, and college—and we will discuss the advantages, disadvantages, and important lessons at each level.

Elementary School

Elementary sports programs are usually not as intense or demanding as parent-run programs because school officials are first interested in education, with extracurricular activities as a secondary priority. Elementary teachers are trained to educate, not to coach. However, they are asked to supervise after-school programs even though many of them have little expertise in sports. Some do it because of the extra stipend that comes with it. Others do it because they know the programs are good for the children.

Conflict surfaces because many don't put as much time and energy into their coaching as the "gung-ho" parental coaches. The overall program at the elementary level is "low-key." As a result, parents think school officials are not interested in their youth. This is not true. School officials see the sports programs from a different perspective, that is, one program that contributes to the overall development of the child. Parents need to understand the total school program so that they can support it and work with school officials to make it complementary to the youth programs sponsored outside the school.

The major advantage of having your child in the elementary school program is that those in charge usually know children. They may not know as much about sports or be as intense or emphasize winning and losing, but they are around children all day. They have been professionally trained to teach children. They apparently like children. Though it is not necessarily true that all elementary coaches will be kind and understanding, your child's chance of getting a tyrant is less than in a parent-run program.

In addition to that, as a taxpayer and a school patron, you have a stronger voice of opposition if you don't like the way your child is being coached in an elementary school program. You can always go to the principal.

Usually, school programs match contestants by age levels. As long as fourth-graders play fourth-graders, there may not be as much size variation as there is in some parent-run programs.

Finally, participating in an elementary school program with classmates could have some educational benefits for your child. Sports provide an opportunity for friendships to grow, and children who are comfortable and at ease among their classmates are likely to learn better and enjoy school more.

Junior High

Probably the most misunderstood level of competition is junior high. Generally speaking, this is the first time that youngsters are involved in interscholastic competition. As with the elementary level, junior-high school officials want to make certain that athletic programs do not overshadow academic programs. Because of this, most school officials operate a limited schedule of contests. Many times, parents feel a lack of emphasis at this level. This may be true in some cases.

Even though the level of competition in junior high is greater than elementary school, the quality of coaching is not always better. Once again, teachers are pushed into coaching because of the pressure to have the sport. Some do an adequate job of supervising and an inadequate job of coaching.

What can you as a parent do about this situation? One answer is to lobby for your school board to hire competent coaches as well as teachers. Lobby for your school board to pay higher salaries to attract better people. If your junior-high coaches are doing a good job, let them know that you appreciate their efforts. There are some who are dedicated to being outstanding coaches at this level.

Another conflict that arises at this level is how much control the high-school coach has over the junior-high program. There needs to be a continuity developed between the junior-high program and the high-school program. In most cases, a solid program takes several years to develop. It is important that parents understand that sometimes the high-school coaches dictate what happens at the junior-high level. Consider the following story as an illustration.

Glenn was a six-foot, 145-pound quarterback on the eighth-grade football team. As a seventh-grader, he had been the starting quarterback, and the team had been undefeated. So you can see he was anticipating an exciting season. But even before the first game, he was moved to a second team behind a good, all-around athlete who could have played several different positions. Because of his size and movement, Glen could only play quarterback. He was, however, an excellent passer. The coaches would only play him on passing downs, which put him at a disadvantage.

No explanation was given to Glen about why the change was made. His father was concerned, so he talked with the junior-high coach. The coach informed Glen's father that he was following the instructions of the high-school coach (who was new that year) to play the other boy. Glen quit the team and never played again.

Who was right? It was a difficult situation. But it was not an unusual happening. Parents need to be aware of this and ready to cope with it. Can the child participate at the Y or at church? Can a new sport be picked up?

Finances are always a problem at the junior-high level. Facilities are often old and outdated. Equipment is "hand-me-down." This is a difficult situation for the youth as well as the parents to accept after being exposed to the finest of facilities and equipment in their youth programs sponsored by outside sources.

A great improvement could be made in this area if schools and communities worked together. I have some advice to give here: School officials, don't be so proud and haughty that you can't accept financial help from patrons. This can be done without losing control. Parents, find out the problems confronted by schools in the area of finance. Give them your financial and physical work support. But at the same time, don't expect that your support will give you the authority to run the program; that is the responsibility of the school. There is so much potential to develop sound programs for junior-high-school students if everyone cooperates and contributes. And the children are the ones who benefit.

High School

To cover this level of competition thoroughly would take more chapters than can be allowed in this book. My attempt will be to highlight a few areas of common interest to all: being cut from the team, serving others (teamwork), having an area of specialization, and handling winning and losing.

Cuts

For the first time, the athlete faces the possibility of being "cut" from the team. To determine whether or not this should happen is not an objective of this book. The simple fact is that it does happen. How you deal with it as a parent is very important in the growth of your child. You can say the coach doesn't know what he is doing, doesn't like your child, is influenced by others in his decisions, or many other things, any one of which may be true. However, what good does that do for the child? It may only feed the desire to look for excuses rather than face the reality of such a decision.

Be positive in your approach. Encourage your child to practice to get better in order to make the team the next season. Encourage other pursuits if the child is lacking in ability. Encourage acceptance of the decision and support for those who made it. This is an opportunity for you as a parent to help your child grow. It is an important learning experience. Sooner or later, we are all faced with decisions like this one. A former president of a small Texas college put it this way: "Adversity causes some men to break; others to break records." Analyze this and see how you as a parent can be instrumental in leading your child during this time of frustration. The child will take on your attitude most often.

Mr. Joe Earl told me the following about what it meant to him to be cut from the high-school basketball team:

> My first love was basketball. I discovered this game at the young age of ten or eleven, and it became for me a cure-all. Belonging to the grade-school basketball club gave me a sense of belonging, and I received attention I had

never had before. I had friends and a sense of well-being that accompanies most sports activities. As a starting member of the team (in those days, more emphasis was placed on the first five), I had a feeling of pride and importance. These emotional feelings were of utmost importance to my well-being at this stage. Coming from a broken home, I was a product of insecurity and emotional upheaval; however, basketball filled a void. I was relatively happy due to this sport, and literally speaking, it was my first love. The honeymoon with basketball lasted until my freshman year in high school.

My first rude awakening was due to the competition that high school brought with it. We had three grade schools feeding into the high school, and I became a victim of numbers—more and better skilled athletes. I still managed to make the freshman team, but my status was relegated to keeping the bench warm with very minimal playing time. Although disappointed at being placed in this role, I remained somewhat content because I was still part of something. I still had a feeling of belonging, and I maintained this position through my sophomore year.

It was my junior year that the world came to an end. I was cut. The basketball team was trimmed to accommodate twelve players on the roster, and I was not one of them. To express how I felt at this time, what my thoughts were, is beyond my capacity. I do know that I acquired an "I don't care" attitude at this time. I could have cared less if the school had been closed down. It had not become apparent to me that one attended school for other reasons than sports, and I was not emotionally prepared for this setback.

My grades began to slide at this time, as did my social life, and I was one unhappy young man. I felt I had lost most of my friends; I was no longer very popular with my fellow classmates; and my life as a whole was pure misery. I do need to say that I recovered a minute amount of self-esteem when as a senior, I was a member of the football team. I never acquired the feeling of well-being that was associated with basketball. There are two reasons for this. One, in my home town, basketball was the leading fan participation sport, and two, our football team had a losing record my senior year (3-5-1).

Reflecting to those days and time, it is quite difficult to see how or what I could have done differently to have avoided this very emotional upheaval. Maybe it was unavoidable (like the measles), and maybe a more secure home life would have softened the shock, and maybe I should not have placed all my eggs in one basket (no pun intended). Perhaps other social interests would have helped.

I do feel that one needs to have balance in his or her life and perhaps maintaining this balance is what life is all about.

The balance to which Joe referred is what the parent must seek in dealing with this emotional struggle. It would be better if both parents were involved. In Joe's case, being from a broken home, this was impossible. However, we know that today approximately 50 percent of marriages are ending in divorce. We also know that most of the time, the children live with the mother. So this puts much of the responsibility on mothers.

Mothers, you need to follow your child's progress and experiences in sports so that you can be of help when the child encounters a problem. Do see that the child has another interest, or help to develop another interest in the event of a "cut" or drop.

Teamwork

High school is the age at which athletes become most competitive. It is very important that they learn the meaning of teamwork—that they learn to put others first. Sometimes, this is difficult to do. An athlete must learn to ask, "Is it really important how many points *I* can score, or is it more important how many points the *team* scores?"

What a tremendous opportunity you have in this area, parents. We really do need one another. All human relationships are based on this concept. Henry J. Kaiser, a man who amassed a fortune during the first half of the century, listed one of his keys to success as the desire to serve others. He said that the more people who benefit from a person's efforts, the better it is for that person, too. I am sure you will agree that it is obvious to us to pick out those who are willing to serve. Quality teams are made up of unselfish players. It is contagious—catch it!

The greatest single sacrifice for the betterment of the team that I have witnessed was made by a young man who played for me. Nick was a five-foot-eight, 141-pound quarterback/defensive back. He was going to be a senior. He had been a part-time starter on defense and a backup quarterback. Our two previous quarterbacks had been excellent. Even though he was very small, I felt Nick would be outstanding because he was intelligent. He worked harder during the summer than the previous two quarterbacks had. I thought he was ready as preseason practice started.

After three days of practice, Nick said he wanted to talk to me. "Coach," he said, "I think we would be a better football team if you would move Steve to the number one quarterback and play me at free safety. I think we can win our first two games while Steve is gaining experience, and then we'll be better the rest of the season with him as quarterback. Maybe I can help the defense."

Steve was a sophomore with no previous experience, but he had a lot of natural ability if he could control his immaturity and inexperience. I told Nick I didn't want to do that and I doubted if the team would accept a sophomore. Nick replied, "Let me talk with the team—it'll be all right."

We made the change and we did win our first two games. We went on to have a perfect season, 10–0. The real reason was the way we played defense under the leadership of Nick who was named all-stater as the smallest defensive back. It was obvious that Nick was a team player who was willing to give up the glory and glamor of the quarterback position to make the team stronger.

Specialization

There are many theories concerning specialization. We have been taught to be well-rounded individuals. It is our belief that athletes should be allowed to participate in as many activities as they can handle. The problem in high-school athletics today is the coach who sees only one sport as being important. This is an area in which parents need to be aware. More and more high-school coaches want their athletes to specialize in one sport. Sometimes this is caused by the pressure put on the coach by the community. Sometimes it is caused by an ego problem.

It is the opinion of most educators that the athlete should have a choice of activities without being pressured by a coach to specialize. The athlete should have the opportunity to participate in multiple sports if he or she has the ability.

Todd was an exceptional athlete in high school. His basketball coach wanted him to devote his time and efforts to basketball. Todd wanted to participate in football, basketball, and track and had the ability to do so. The problem was solved when Todd's parents moved to another city where he became all-state in football, outstanding in basketball, and a state champion hurdler in track. He received a scholarship in football, not basketball. In this case, the coach was unfair to Todd. His parents made a decision that was in Todd's best interest. High-school athletics are for the athlete, not the coach or the parent.

Winning and Losing

Parents, you have a most important role in dealing with your child's response to winning and losing. This might be the best lesson that can be learned from participating in athletics. No doubt, it is an experience that will be replayed many times in life.

As a coach, I learned from my son an important lesson about losing. After a Friday-night football game in which his team lost, I met him at home. Unfortunately, my team had lost also. After discussing the games, some of his friends came over to the house, and within thirty minutes they were laughing and having a good time. You see, the game was over. They had played hard and lost, and that wasn't going to change. Yet they continued to enjoy their companionship and life went on. I used to replay lost games all weekend, hoping the results might change. We should never lose sight of the fact that a game is only a game.

Just as we should not allow ourselves to be too upset over losing, we should never take winning as the only thing. What is most important and lasting is what happened in the process of the victory. Who remembers the score? I'm not saying that winning is not important, because it is. What I am saying is that it must have meaning. In this context, losing is also important. Learning to handle both experiences positively makes us better individuals. As parents we can help our young athletes to move in that direction.

Junior College

Junior colleges have developed so much recently and offer the young athlete so many opportunities that they deserve some of your attention, particularly if you have a young athlete nearing the end of a high-school career.

Junior-college programs can be put into one of two broad classes. Some are designed for the young athlete who wants to play a couple more years before quitting competition altogether. On the other hand, some junior colleges are stepping stones to major universities and lucrative scholarships. The differences between these two are determined by the commitment of the school and the quality of the coaches. With a little investigation, you should be able to tell what kind of program a school has. But be careful, frequently junior colleges choose to emphasize one sport, sometimes at the expense of the rest.

Good junior-college programs usually have good results in placing their graduating athletes in major college programs. Some major colleges recruit heavily from junior colleges. Knowing this, you will want to ask, "What kind of an athlete would be advised to attend a junior-college stepping-stone program?" The following types seem to be most suited for such programs:

1. *The young athlete who may have trouble with college academics.* Usually, junior colleges are smaller and more personal than major uni-

versities and the teachers are more sensitive to student anxieties. I don't mean to imply that the work is easier or the standards lower. They may or may not be, but there is a greater chance that the instruction will be more sensitive to the student than in a larger university.

2. *The young athlete who is almost good enough but who needs to grow or perfect some skills.* Junior-college competition will allow this young person to develop in a solid program without having to spend a couple of years in the shadows of a horde of gifted athletes at the major university. Some people have a rather rapid growth spurt somewhere between eighteen and twenty years of age, and junior college may give the late grower a chance to develop physically.

3. *The young athlete who is confused by all the recruiting hassle and needs some time to reflect before jumping into a major program.* Usually, the junior college coaches can be a big asset in helping that young athlete choose the right university.

4. *The young athlete who wants to play close enough to home to allow the family to watch and the junior college is the only thing that close.*

College

Although there are not as many opportunities to play college sports as there are to play high-school sports, there are enough opportunities to encourage any young athlete who has the interest and ability to investigate the possibilities for college participation. If your athlete is thinking about a full-ride scholarship that is going to finance all of college and life ever after, you both may be terribly disappointed. But if what is wanted is a chance to play, there may be plenty of opportunities, particularly if the college is chosen carefully.

There are six divisions of college competition. Two major organizations certify, promote, support, and control college sports. The biggest and best known is the National Collegiate Athletic Association or NCAA. When schools voluntarily join the NCAA, all their programs come under NCAA supervision.

There are four major divisions in NCAA depending on such things as school size and program concentration. Those divisions include Division IA (the biggies), Division IAA (those schools just under the biggies but still big), Division II (smaller than IAA but still large enough to be on the map), Division III (small colleges). Although the NCAA has some universal rules, the organization also provides specific grade rules, recruitment rules, and scholarship rules for each of the divisions.

The other major organization that certifies, promotes, and controls college sports is the National Association of Interscholastic Athletics, or NAIA. This organization has a Division One and a Division Two, depending on the size and quality of the school and program. It also has specific rules for such things as recruitment, scholarships, and grades.

If your young athlete is interested in a specific college program, you will want to ask first, "What organization and what division is this college in?" After you get that information, you can then check into the specific rules and opportunities that affiliation carries.

Regardless of whether the college athlete receives a large scholarship, sports participation still offers those values and lessons I mentioned in the high-school section. And it is this opportunity for positive and meaningful experiences that makes sports a worthwhile learning experience for any person who chooses to participate.

During this time when schools are on tight money budgets, many are asking if extracurricular sports really belong in a school program. To veteran coaches who have coached and watched thousands of young people grow into maturity through school programs, the answer is obvious. Sports teach us how to balance our lives, how to manage our time, how to accept the consequences of our own efforts. In schools, sports become a rallying point, a focus, a center of school prestige. Frequently, sports give schools their character, and a good sports program contributes to the whole educational image of the school. Any teacher who has been in this situation will say that the easiest, most productive years to teach math or English are those years when one of the major sports teams wins a state championship.

Since schools have been given the primary responsibility of providing sports opportunities for this nation's young people, to decrease the emphasis on sports in schools is to decrease sports opportunities for our young people. The critics must understand this. Unlike other countries, our society provides only limited participation for young people outside of schools.

For these reasons, we encourage you, both as parents and as sports enthusiasts, to take a firm stand on the educational value of sports and to support your school program.

What Parents Ask

1. *My daughter just got cut from the freshman basketball team. What should we do?*

First, keep her spirits up. After that, you can take one of two actions. You can either forget basketball or encourage her to practice and play and take every chance to improve. Those freshman girls are going to encounter many body changes before their senior year. Your daughter could become the best one yet, if she keeps her interest up.

2. *Our junior high school just dropped its interscholastic competitive program. Will this hurt our athletes' chances?*

Wow, that is a hot issue right now with all the money problems schools have. But the answer to your question depends on several factors.
A. How good was the junior-high program to start with?
B. With what is the school going to replace the interscholastic program? (Some intramural programs could even be an improvement over some weak interscholastic programs.)
C. What will the high school do to compensate? Some high schools are adding summer programs and other programs that will give those incoming players an advantage.

3. *What do I do if I don't like the way the coach is handling my athlete?*

That's simple. Go see the coach, but keep the meeting at a professional level. Just remind him that you have a disagreement. Point out your side and listen carefully to his side. Don't lose your temper. Don't become defensive. Talk like adults. Perhaps the two of you can reach an agreement. If not, you then have to decide if the coach's position is damaging your athlete. If it isn't, forget it. Whatever you do, don't criticize the coach in front of your athlete. A coach is no better than the respect his athletes have for him. If you destroy your athlete's respect for the coach, you will hurt your athlete yourself.

17. *Scholarships and Other Myths*

The other day, one of the wags down at the coffee shop announced proudly that his daughter had just won a two-hundred-dollar scholarship to study piano in college. I asked about the application process. What he told me provides an interesting commentary on a rather strange contemporary notion. He loaded the family into the station wagon, drove two hundred miles one way, and stayed in a motel overnight so his daughter could play in front of a group of judges the next day. But at least, she won a scholarship!

That kind of attitude is really saying that regardless of what it takes, what it costs, what it is for, one must receive a scholarship to finance one's way through college. When we put that notion in perspective, we can really see it as a silly idea, and we college coaches probably see the silliness before anyone else.

We understand that some students really do need the money to get through college. We know that not all families can spend three hundred dollars earning a two-hundred-dollar scholarship, but let's accept the first guiding principle of college scholarships, particularly of athletic scholarships.

There Ain't No Free Lunch

You and your potential college athlete need to come to grips with this statement before you go on with this chapter and before you start entertaining the notion of winning a college athletic scholarship. If your son or daughter wins a college scholarship, even a big one, that athlete will invest hundreds and hundreds of hours of hard work earning that money. When it is all over, it might have been easier and more financially sound to have worked those hours in an outside job. Of course, the athlete has the privilege of investing those hours in something enjoyable, but don't miss the point. Athletic scholarships are not gifts. They are exchanges for hard work.

This isn't the place to correct all the false notions about college finances, but do keep in mind that colleges are actively recruiting students, whether or not they can play football. If your college-age offspring has the desire and the ability to get a college education, there are lots of ways to get there even without one of those coveted scholarships. Winning an athletic scholarship is not the life-or-death matter some students and parents have made it out to be.

But if a scholarship is what you really want, let's talk about how you can get one. To achieve this, we will look at three topics: the scholarship chase, what your athlete needs from you, and what to do if the athlete doesn't get a scholarship.

The Scholarship Chase

If you and your young athlete decide to try for a college scholarship, you need to know that your odds aren't very good. Very few high-school athletes win college grants. But some do, so there is some hope. To make the most of that hope, you need to understand as much as you can about how the recruitment process works. If you are not careful, you and your athlete could get so caught up in the recruitment process that you forget that there will be a college education plus four years of playing experience to follow that decision.

Most college coaches like to receive lots of names, and they get those names from several sources. They search the newspaper to see what young athletes are doing well. They clip all-conference and all-state rosters. They attend games. They watch films. Some high-school coaches send around a list of all their seniors. Alumni and supporters make recommendations.

From this broad list of names, the coaches begin the recruiting procedure. They send letters to everybody. Sometimes these are congratulatory notes on a fine performance or just "get-acquainted" notes. But thousands of high-school athletes get these letters. This doesn't mean that the college is actually recruiting everybody. They are just gathering evidence and putting together a list.

Now the coach begins to gather data in earnest. To get this information, he will probably contact the high-school coach and the athlete.

During this time, the coach is also evaluating the source of the information he is getting. For example, most college coaches accept some reports as slight exaggerations. If the athlete ran a 4.5-second forty-yard dash in high school, he might run a 4.7 in the college test.

The coach is also getting some information about the athlete's academic ability and is evaluating that information against material about how good that high school is and what those grades really mean. This doesn't mean that good athletes with low grades don't get recruited. We know they do. We have heard those stories, but good athletes with good high-school grades have more options. If they can handle their college classwork, they present one less problem to the harried coaches.

At this stage, the coach may ask for game films or may go watch the young athlete play. Again, this still doesn't mean that the athlete is being recruited; it just means that the coach is interested.

Now that the coach has contacted the athlete twice and has gathered a full sheet of data, he evaluates all this and makes some decisions about which athletes he will pursue and with what intensity. In fact, many coaches at this stage have ranked their prospects beginning with number one and going through the list. Decisions have to be based on several factors, including how many scholarships they have available and what kinds of players they need. (For example, a basketball team may have an abundance of centers but needs guards. In this case, your six-foot-nine son will not be one of the top players on the list. It doesn't mean that he isn't college material. It just means that this school doesn't have a scholarship slot for him.) Of course, exceptional athletes are on everyone's list despite the need.

When the coaches have narrowed the list to those prospects they want, they begin the hard sell. The hard sell takes one of two forms. The coach or a recruiter may visit the athlete, the parents, and the high-school officials. Or the college may invite the athlete to come to campus at college expense. At this stage, the major universities are limited by NCAA regulations about the number of visits both ways. This is not yet a scholarship offer but only a pledge of interest. Only about one-third of the high-school athletes who visit campuses are offered scholarships, but it does indicate that someone is interested. And this leads us to the second point.

Parental Leadership and Counsel

The process can become intensely confusing at this point. Your wise counsel and cool head will be needed. You can actually prepare for this time by making sure you have established a working relationship with your high-school senior before you get to this point. Show beforehand that you respect your child's judgment and that you are interested in helping to make the decisions the young person really wants to make. Make it clear you are available to talk seriously and honestly. There are several areas in which you can provide parental leadership and counsel.

1. Don't let that young athlete and student become so involved in the future that the ability to enjoy the present is forgotten. Being young has an added burden of having to wonder what the next step of life is going to bring. All high-school seniors fall into this, but the young athlete being courted by several colleges at the same time is particularly vulnerable. Everybody is giving constant reminders about how it is going to be somewhere else next year. Everybody wants forms filled out, letters written, recommendations, films, and statistics sent. But in the middle of all this, the athlete still has to play basketball each evening and study for the English literature test.

Recruiting trips to the college can be devastating. Once on campus, your young athlete is going to get a taste of the finest and best of college life. Dirty laundry, term paper assignments, all-night study times, and the size of the chemistry book will certainly not be part of the campus tour. That trip may make high school look like nothing but hard, boring work in comparison with the exciting possibilities of campus life. Beware!

2. Help your student go through the process of selecting a college as if athletics were not a factor. Make sure to deal with questions such as a major area of study and the quality of the school. Help your athlete get the upper hand and make a list of colleges narrow enough to handle while the coaches are making theirs. This will reduce the pressure when recruiters begin to call and will make it easier for you to keep your child's mind on high school.

3. Remember that the college recruiter is just another door-to-door salesman. Treat him as such. You could put on a clean tablecloth and lay out the good china, but always question his motives and make sure you and your young athlete ask the right questions. And what are they?

How many of your scholarship athletes graduate and how long does it take them? After all, the young person is going for a college degree and not just to play a sport. Whatever you do, ask that question first. It will reveal a lot of information: What does the coach think of academics?

What does the college think of its athletes? How important are classes? How good are the students on the team who will be your athlete's best friends? How demanding is the sport schedule?

What happens to the scholarship if your young athlete gets sick or hurt and can't play any longer? Ask the question and ask for *evidence.* If a recruiter promises your athlete something, ask him to put it in writing. You can tell him that you trust him, but a recruiter can get fired or die. Who keeps his promises when he is not around?

How many games will I get to see? You may not want to ask the recruiter that question, but you and your athlete need to ask it of each other. One of the joys of having an athlete in the family is having the opportunity to see the performance. You need to consider this as your athlete makes this important decision.

What does the scholarship offer in dollar amounts? This is particularly necessary when the college offers portions of scholarships so that they can spread their money further.

You can add your own questions about such things as living facilities, laundry facilities, majors, equipment, and time commitments. The preceding questions are a few you might not have thought about.

4. Don't let your young athlete put all hopes and plans in the scholarship basket. Scholarships sometimes fall through. I visited an athlete who went through this process and in the end was not offered a scholarship. He was so hurt that he was thinking of quitting athletics. His parents were of no help to him because they were not aware of the process. As a parent you need to learn as much about recruiting as you can so that you can counsel your child throughout the process.

End of the Chase

What do you do if your young athlete doesn't get the scholarship? Well, you send him or her to college as if the scholarship had been received, and you encourage participation in the sport anyway, particularly if the reason for wanting to participate was enjoyment. College recruiters are not infinitely wise. They miss as many and perhaps more than they hit. Encourage him or her to go to a college where he or she can participate. Many times this will be a smaller college where the caliber of competition is better than what most people think. Many young people are still growing at that age, and they may change as their bodies develop. A few years ago, we had an all-conference defensive safety on our college team. As a high-school senior, that same young man was good enough to go down on the kick-off team and that is all. He didn't even win a legitimate letter his senior year in high school. But four years later we were really glad we had him, and our opponents stood around wondering how they had missed him in the recruiting process.

If sports have value, their value is more important than the dollars of a scholarship. Don't be caught up in the American myth.

What Parents Ask

1. *I think my son is being overlooked for a college scholarship. How can I attract some attention?*

   Well, you can put together a resume of statistics such as size, speed, and grades and send them in yourself. But if you think your son deserves a scholarship, convince him to go to college without one and walk on. If he is good enough to play, those coaches will see him.

2. *Do female athletes have as many chances for scholarships as the guys?*

   There aren't as many women players in college sports, so there won't be as many scholarships, but good female athletes are heavily recruited and get good scholarships. If your daughter is good enough to play college sports, someone will want her.

3. *How important are grades?*

   In spite of what you might have heard about college athletes and academics, grades are a factor. Regardless of how good an athlete is, he or she has to stay eligible. Coaches like to brag about their athletes' academic achievements. If your athlete can help bring up the team average, that will make the coach happy. The great players are going to get offers even if their grades aren't great, but if two athletes of equal ability are competing for the same scholarship, the offer will go to the athlete with the best grades.

18. *Intramurals*

By now you should be convinced that one of the first purposes of participating in sports is to have a good time, that sports participation can teach us some worthwhile lessons that we may have trouble getting somewhere else, and that if sports participation is valuable for one child, it is valuable for all children.

But if you have been convinced of these points, your next question should be, "Where does my child get those kinds of opportunities?" In recent years, some schools have attempted to answer that question and that need by developing well-defined, well-organized intramural programs that are open to all students who wish to participate.

Although there are a few intramural programs in elementary schools and a few more in high schools around the country, these programs have become increasingly popular at the junior-high level, particularly in those communities where competitive junior-high sports have been de-emphasized and even eliminated during this age of budget crunches and demands for higher educational standards. These programs are also very popular in many colleges. For example, in our college, more than 50 percent of our student body participates in the intramural basketball program during the winter.

The purpose of an intramural program is to offer participation opportunity to the greatest number of people at the lowest possible cost. Usually, the school will assign one or two staff members to organize and operate the intramural programs. The students who register to play either form their own teams from among their friends or they are assigned to teams by the directors who try to achieve some balance of ability.

Games are scheduled into school facilities when those facilities are not being used by someone else. There is almost no coaching, very little practicing, and very little physical conditioning. Sometimes the level of competition, if not organized, is nonetheless intense. Since many of these players are not experienced athletes who have been trained mentally as well as physically for competition, they sometimes have problems adjusting to the demands and frustrations of competition, so they play more emotionally than varsity players.

Regardless of the level of organization and the quality of play, some schools have found that their intramural programs provide a valuable service for their students and the school. Let's look at some of those.

Values

1. The intramural program offers the thrills and lessons of competition to anyone who chooses to participate.

2. Intramural programs offer a large number of students something to do in their spare time. This is particularly valuable for those who don't have the time or interest to devote a major part of their lives to the training and practice needed to participate on the varsity level.

3. Intramural programs offer young athletes an opportunity to explore several sports while they are making a choice about specializing. Although these athletes won't get much coaching, they should at least get a taste for the game and some idea about their ability to perform that particular sport.

4. Joining an intramural team can offer some youngsters the same sense of community or belonging that any other team membership offers. I have seen situations where a junior-high-school student uses intramural team membership as a chief source of personal identification. He belongs to the team so he at least belongs to something. You may argue that this is a rather flimsy self-identity, and I agree. But it is better than having no sense of identity at all.

5. Since intramurals are usually after school or in the evening, these programs open the school facilities for student use for longer periods of time, and that is smart economics. If the taxpayers in a school district go to the trouble and expense of building a gym, that gym should be used as much as possible.

6. Intramural programs are inexpensive to operate. One or two directors can run a program for hundreds of players.

7. Although intramural programs are not often highly structured or controlled, they are usually better controlled than the after-school play-

ground games and thus offer the athlete some representation of the real thing.

8. Intramurals offer the young athlete who has been cut from the varsity an opportunity to perfect skills in order to try for the school team again next year. I once coached in a school where about half our high-school varsity basketball players came from the junior-high team, but the other half came out of the junior-high intramural program. If we had not had that program in that school, those players probably would have lost interest, dropped out, and never realized their athletic success. The community would have missed the joy of watching them play. Our varsity basketball was quite successful, partly because of the junior-high intramural program.

As you can see from this list, a good intramural program can offer your budding young athlete several values, but as with all good things, there are some warnings. Let me list some of those.

Cautions

1. Most of the time there is little or no coaching. If your child chooses to participate in the intramural program, learning the sport and improving will have to be done without that help. One of the big dangers of this lack of coaching is that a young player can develop bad habits of performance or even a bad attitude, so you may want to spend enough time with your child out in the backyard to make sure some wrong moves are not being picked up.

2. The players don't get much help on learning how to cope with competition. Every good coach spends about as much time teaching players how to handle competition as he does teaching them the game. Again, you may have to help. If your child is participating, act interested. Ask about the team success. Ask what your child is learning. Through those questions, you will be opening the door for communication in case something is bothering the child about the nature of competition. If so, you may need to counsel. I also would recommend that you show up for one of the games and watch the child play, but do that only if other parents are. Don't embarrass your child by being the only parent who has ever shown up in the history of the intramural program.

3. Frequently, the game officiating is as casual as the playing, and it is quite easy for young players to develop the debilitating habit of blaming their performance on referees. This kind of attitude will not only

corrupt a good athlete, but it will corrupt anybody in any endeavor. If you see this kind of attitude developing in your child, do something to correct it.

4. The facilities are not always available at the most convenient times. If your child participates in intramurals, you may find yourself in the transportation business at some rather odd times of the day or night. But you always have to measure the commitment you have to make against the values your child is getting from sports participation. I really hope rewards justify your efforts.

5. Varsity athletes may use the intramural program as a cheap out. Let's suppose I am a fifteen-year-old girl trying out for the varsity basketball team. The practices are long and hard. We have to do tons of sit-ups, and I hate sit-ups. We run fundamental drills by the hours. Regardless of how hard I try, the coach is never satisfied with my performance. She tells me that I have ability and she is just trying to get me to perform at my level. With all that practice and hard work, we rarely scrimmage in practice. I see my friends having a good time in the intramural program. They are playing full games twice a week, and they don't have to do sit-ups. It would be so easy for me to quit the varsity and join an intramural team. I could be one of the best and never have to worry about my potential. "What is wrong with that?" you may ask.

As you know by now, I am all in favor of letting athletes make some of their own decisions, but I am also in favor of their getting some counsel from parents and coaches. In this case, the athlete needs advice. Any decision that is made from a lack of integrity or a lack of persistence is a bad decision. The fun of sports is a long-range goal as well as an immediate feeling. If this girl can muster the discipline to stay on the varsity team, her long-range happiness will be far greater than anything she receives from intramurals.

6. Your child's school doesn't have an intramural program. Now, that is a real hardship, but it could be corrected. Public schools belong to the taxpayers, and they are usually open to fulfilling the educational needs of students. If you and several other parents feel that an intramural sports program would fulfill an educational need for many children at the school, contact the school officials. Start with the athletic director or building principal. If you can convince one of those officials to join your side, you will have a much stronger voice when you pull out the big guns.

Be prepared to answer three objections the school officials are going to submit. (1) The school cannot afford to hire the supervisors. (2) The school does not have enough facilities. (3) There is not enough interest. But if you believe that your child needs the values and the fun of participating in sports and can't get the opportunity anywhere else in the community, you should be creative and persuasive in helping the school officials find working solutions to those problems.

What Parents Ask

1. *I don't want my son to become competitive, but I would like him to learn sports. Wouldn't intramurals be his best choice?*

   Maybe, but probably not. Some intramural games are really cut-throat. Usually, learning to handle competition is learned from experience.

2. *When is it economically feasible for a school to start an intramural program?*

   I wouldn't dare to tell any school how to run its budget. But if a school does not run enough interscholastic programs to accommodate most of the people who want to participate, the intramural program could be a good solution. If you think your school needs a program because you know the people who would participate, see the athletic director or principal.

3. *How do you classify church-league programs?*

   Church-league programs vary from being almost as organized as school varsity programs to being looser in structure than intramurals. If your athlete is in a church-league program, you will want to monitor that experience closely. He or she may be learning great stuff.

19. *Sports Camps*

Going to camp has become something of a summer ritual for thousands of children throughout the country. Private camps, specialized camps, church camps, and scout camps all promise a unique experience vital to a child's growth and development. Children trudge off to camp with their suitcases stuffed with comic books and cut-off jeans, and they come home with tales of short-sheeting the counselor's bed, catching snakes and poison ivy, chasing the camp ghost into the woods, and eating terrible food.

In recent years, some enterprising coaches and promoters have thrown a basketball into the middle of all that and have invented the sports camp. This enterprise has introduced parents to yet another decision in that long line of earth-shaking decisions required of all interested parents. As a parent, you probably have a whole list of questions you would like to ask about sports camps, such as, "Will I cheat my child out of something if I don't send him?" "Is camp worth the sacrifice of money and time?" "Will she learn anything?" "How do I pick the right camp?" In this chapter, I am going to try to answer all those questions by concentrating on the one question—"When is sports camp worth my money and my child's time and when is it not?" To help you find the answer for your particular situation, I am going to present you with a list of questions only you can answer.

What Kind of Child Do You Have?

Since I run a specific football camp, I make my money by convincing parents that they have to send their young athletes to me for a couple of weeks every year. And I can be quite convincing because if I am not, I go broke. But we both know that my camp is not for everybody. Anybody who doesn't have those special talents and dreams my camp will nurture will be unhappy at my camp.

Regardless of whether it is a camp or a clinic, a day camp or a residence camp, a specialized camp or a general sports camp, a sports camp is about sports. The campers will be instructed in sports, will play sports, practice sports, and dream about sports and sports heroes at night. If your child enjoys whittling and crafts and chasing snakes in the forest more than sports, choose another kind of camp. You will be doing everybody a favor.

When the time comes for you and your child to choose a camp, listen to the people down the street, talk to the relatives and coaches, read all the literature, but make the final decision based on your child's interests and aptitudes and abilities. Since only you and the child have that kind of information, you must assume responsibility for that decision.

What Kind of Camp Is It?

Once you have decided that your child would enjoy a sports camp, you have begun your research. You now have to decide on what kind of camp is best for your child. Since you have so many options here, I provide you with a list.

1. The General Sports Camp

When I was younger, I worked for several summers in a general sports camp. Although we were a rather expensive camp, we had our campers for twenty-six days and we offered a counselor-camper ratio of one to eight. During that twenty-six-day session, we offered instruction and competition in baseball, basketball, volleyball, wrestling, soccer, tennis, archery, golf, swimming, rowing, diving, and riflery. Some campers were allowed to concentrate a bit in one particular sport, but all received limited instruction and participation in all sports offered.

That general approach was excellent for the athletes of average ability or interest. They received good instruction and enough competition to help them develop their skills in a wide variety of sports. During the session, we observed good growth in both skill and attitude in most of the campers in most of the sports. But since not one camper ever spent all the time in any one sport, we never got into the really fine points of skill development or technique. If a boy had been primarily interested in developing himself in a single sport such as basketball, he would have been better off at a good basketball camp than at our place. On the other hand, this generalized sports camp is ideal for the young person who has a good interest in sports but still is in the process of experimenting to make a decision.

2. The Specialized Sports Camp

I now run a specialized sports camp in two states every summer. It is a football camp. For one week young men who come to my camp play football. Oh, we stop once in awhile to eat and sleep, but mostly we play football. But to be more specific, my camp is for quarterbacks, receivers, and defensive backs. We don't just play football; we pass the football, we catch the football, and we try to keep other people from catching the football. That is about all we do, day in and day out. If your child isn't interested in catching, passing, or knocking down footballs, he really shouldn't come to my camp.

On the other hand, if he is interested in one of those activities, my specialized camp could really help him. We have excellent coaches who know what they are doing in those specific skills. We have a sound philosophy of the football passing game which has been proved in competition (our college team has led the nation in our division of competition each of the three seasons I have been a college coach). We know what we are doing, and we teach those young campers the skills and techniques that will give them the edge in competition on their school teams.

One year at our football camp, we observed the progress that three athletes from the same school made. They were from a very small school in Illinois. Compared to the majority of the athletes in the camp, they were inferior in talent. Yet each of those players improved according to his own ability. What those three players accomplished was to win the state championship in the Class A level and set records for their school.

What I am trying to do here is to give you a picture of what a specialized sports camp does. If your young athlete has already made a choice about a specific sport and a specific role in that sport, the experience and instruction of a specialized camp where friendships develop with other athletes of similar interests and talents and where good, personal coaching is available may be of great value.

Be sure to read the camp promotion material carefully. Some specialized camps are very specialized. One summer we sent our son to a basketball camp where we thought he would get a well-rounded experience. Instead, the camp focused entirely on defensive skills and techniques. He didn't get to shoot a ball the whole week he was there. But I don't blame the camp people. We, as his parents, were to blame for not reading the brochure carefully enough. We made a wrong decision.

Clinics

Some specialized camps are called clinics. Although I am not sure I always know the difference between the two, clinics are frequently traveling camps. A group of experts comes into a community such as a college campus and offers an intense few days of instruction in a particular sport such as running, gymnastics, or soccer. Usually, these experts are well-known athletes in that particular sport. Since they conduct several clinics throughout the summer, they are trained instructors. However, since they do conduct so many clinics and meet so many young campers, they may not build as close a relationship with the campers as some instructors do in some camping situations.

Day Camps

So far I have described resident camps where young athletes leave home for a few days or a few weeks and live at the camp. This kind of camp offers the child a camping experience in addition to good coaching. The athlete has a chance to live with and develop a relationship with other athletes who have the same interests and skills.

For the young athlete who could profit from a sports camp but can't leave home for one reason or another, the day camp provides a great opportunity. The day camp or commuter camp is just that. The camper drives in for instruction and participation for some part of the day. Many young athletes receive valuable instruction and do improve in day camps, particularly if the coaching is good and the coach-athlete ratio is small enough to provide personal instruction. However, the interest level is usually not as intense in day camps as in resident camps simply because there is no off-field instruction such as film sessions or classrooms.

How Do You Evaluate a Camp?

1. Scanning the Litter

Before you start the process of selection, make sure you have information about several options. This decision may be more important than buying a new car. Make sure you do your shopping before you commit yourself to any decision. To get that list, you can ask coaches, particularly the high-school coaches at your school. They usually know the camps that come close to their philosophy, and since your young athlete will probably play for those coaches, your child could get an edge at camp. Consult publications. Write to the national headquarters for the sport your child selects. Ask around. If you know someone who has attended such a camp, ask about that camp.

2. Assessing the Quality

Since your child is going to sports camp to learn sports, the best camp is the one with the best coaches. Most of the time, you can know the head coach or director well enough to make a decision about how good he is. Usually, these people are either coaches or former players, so you can study their philosophies and success records. You can know whether those philosophies are what you want your child to learn.

Regardless of how much influence the director has, he won't coach your child every minute of every day. The next question you have to ask is, "How good are the other coaches?" Since you have no way of getting at that information, you have to settle for another question, "What is the coach-athlete ratio?" If the camp doesn't offer your child more individual coaching than a normal school or parent-run program, you are wasting your money and the athlete's time at that camp. I visited a camp and watched receivers catch passes. The coach-player ratio was so huge that each receiver caught three balls during the thirty minutes I watched. That wasn't fair to anyone.

You also need to be cautious about the "special speakers" some camps use to sell their program. They get your attention by telling you that some well-known sports figure will be there to speak to the campers. Oh, he comes all right, but he makes a little ten-minute speech and goes on his merry way. In the meantime, your child is at that camp for a week, trying to remember if it is worth all this to see a hero at a distance for ten minutes.

Finally, you need to ask, "Is it fun? Will my child have a good time?" Of course, the answer depends a lot on your child. But some camps are designed to provide the campers with a good time so they will leave with a positive attitude, not only about the camp but about the sport in general. That is what a sports camp should achieve. One good way of finding out whether a camp provides that positive experience is to find out how many campers go back year after year. A camp that has a large percentage of its campers repeating is probably a good camp, offering both a good time and good instruction in the sport.

How Much Should You Pay?

Camps vary in price according to the quality of facilities, the quality of food, and the counselor-camper ratio, but you can expect to pay somewhere around two hundred dollars a week for a specialized sports camp. Some are more expensive and some are cheaper. The cost does not necessarily imply quality. You will have to shop for a reasonably priced camp with good quality by asking the same questions covered in the last section.

How Do You Make Sure Your Child Makes the Most of the Camping Experience?

I have a definite recommendation. I make this from the standpoint of a coach, a parent, and a camp director who really enjoys seeing campers apply themselves and make the most of the camping experience. If your child wants to go to a sports camp, make that child pay part of the cost. That will force some commitment to camp before the child even gets there. It will be a personal choice, an investment in the outcome of the camp. At the same time, your child will learn the value of work and money, and your child will be a better person and a better athlete.

What Parents Ask

1. *My daughter plays basketball on her school team. All the other girls on the team are going to basketball camp. But we can't afford it. Will we cheat our daughter by not letting her go?*

Well, you don't have to. Those other girls will receive some personal coaching and a lot of playing time, and that will give them an advantage. If you can provide that kind of attention to your daughter, she could learn just as much at home, but she will still miss the interaction with the other players. Why don't you check to see if there are camp scholarships for your daughter or encourage her to get a job to help pay for part of her way.

2. *My son can't decide between basketball camp, where he doesn't know anybody, or scout camp where his friends are going. How can I help?*

Toss a coin! First make sure he knows what he will be doing at each. At basketball camp, he will play basketball most of the time. If he really enjoys basketball and has some confidence, he should enjoy basketball camp regardless of who is there. But if he isn't that confident and doesn't make friends easily, he could be lonely for awhile. In short sports camps, friendships have to form quickly because there is not much time to let them develop. Usually the most aggressive athletes become the most popular because they are the first noticed.

3. *My daughter wants to go to three different camps this summer. That is all right with us, but will it confuse her to get those different philosophies of coaching?*

No! If she doesn't lose interest or wear out, all that playing time will do her good. Most young people are equipped with an automatic shutoff valve that turns off what they can't handle. Coaches always teach more than athletes can learn!

20. *Private Sports Clubs*

So far I have talked about sports opportunities in parent-run organizations, school programs, including intramurals, and camps and clinics; but there is another form of sports opportunity for children and young people that might appeal to your child, depending on tastes and skills. That is the privately-owned sports club.

Private clubs are usually businesses offering facilities, coaching, instruction, and supervision of competition to its paying customers. Most of these clubs are one-sport enterprises specializing in such things as gymnastics, swimming, tennis, martial arts, weight lifting, diving, ice skating, archery, or riflery. Membership is usually open to anyone who has the money to pay for the service, but some of the better organizations will turn down potential customers who would not profit from instruction in that specific sport.

Frequently, private clubs offer children participation in sports not offered by the school or parent-run organizations. Also, since private clubs usually demand no more than one or two hours per week of the child's time, your child may want to supplement a sports interest with participation in a private club activity. For example, your football-playing son may profit from private lessons in one of the martial arts such as judo or karate; or your basketball-playing daughter might enjoy and profit from private lessons in gymnastics.

These clubs can function as businesses because they offer two basic services—facilities and instruction. They should be evaluated on those terms. Thus, if your young athlete decides that he or she would like to develop skills or compete in one of the sports available in a private club in your community, you will need to make yourself something of an expert in both the sport and the facilities around the sport. Although I can't provide you with all the information you are going to need to become an expert, perhaps in this chapter we can introduce you to the questions you need to ask in order to become knowledgeable enough to help your future Olympian make a decision.

How Do You Find What Is Available?

That is an easy question to answer. Use the Yellow Pages. Look for ads in the newspapers. Consult local school coaches. Write the national association of the sport. Ask your friends. After you have done one or all of the above, ask your child, who probably knows all about every sports opportunity in town.

How Do You Make a Choice?

If you have already read the chapter on camps, you may get the idea that this is a rerun, but the same suggestions do apply in both cases. Since the service the club offers can be divided into facilities and coaching, look at those two factors. Talk to the head coach or director. Check his credentials and reputation. Meet some of the assistants. Ask about the turnover in the coaching staff. If a coaching staff has been together for a few years, they usually like each other, they like kids, and they like the sport. If the coach is happy, your child will probably be happy. If the coach hates his work, your child will probably learn to hate the workout. The coach's attitude is contagious.

Check the coach-athlete ratio. You are paying for individual instruction. Make sure the classes are small enough to permit your child some of the coach's time. A good way to do this is to divide the number of athletes each coach has in a class into the number of minutes the athletes are there. This will give you a formula for determining the exact cost of instruction.

In assessing the facilities, look again at ratio. Will your child have ample time with the equipment? After that, look for safety features. Don't get too carried away with expecting the newest and the best. Creative coaches can achieve more with average equipment than dull coaches can achieve with great equipment.

How Often Do Athletes Attend the Private Clubs?

This depends on the club and the sport available, but an hour a week seems to be something of a standard. Sometimes private clubs schedule free sessions in addition to the scheduled ones so the athletes who want more practice or coaching can come for extra time at odd times during the week.

How Much Can You Expect to Pay?

Again, this varies from club to club and sport to sport, but somewhere between twenty dollars and twenty-five dollars per month seems to be a going rate for many clubs. As I warned about camps, you need to shop for clubs and prices. The most expensive may not always be the best clubs.

How Early Should You Start a Child in a Private Club?

Some of the private clubs, particularly in certain sports, have begun to offer their services to very young children. Many swimming clubs have classes for children as young as two years of age, and some gymnastics clubs offer classes to three-year-olds. Does that mean you should start your child in a private-club sport at that age? You are the only one who can make that decision. Look at all the factors. Does the child have an active play life or is some outside stimulus needed? Is the child mature enough to profit from organized instruction? Does the child need an opportunity for social interaction?

Notice that I have not yet mentioned what *you* might need. Throughout the book, I have promoted the theme that the child ought to be able to make the choice about sports participation. Obviously, a two- or even a three-year-old will not have much voice in that decision. Since at this age, the child has to trust you with that important decision, you really need to be more sensitive and wiser than you will need to be when the child is eight or ten years of age.

In the midst of all this cry for sensitivity, I will make a definite suggestion. If there seems to be a question about whether the child is ready, wait. Wait until you are convinced beyond a doubt that your child is ready. The biggest error we make in starting children into organized sports is that we start them too early. There are a few examples of people who lost a few years because they waited too long, but we have thousands of examples of people who started swimming at three years old and burned out at eight years old.

When Is It Time for the Child to Quit the Private Club?

Notice how I can go right from the subject of burnout to the question about quitting. The two are definitely related. If you are a wise parent, you will learn how to detect your child's rhythms and moods, and you will learn how to distinguish between a permanent mood change and a temporary one. In any sport, your child will have times of greater intensity than others, but you won't want your child to quit just because of a little momentary fatigue. You may want to propose a different practice routine or some variation in other areas.

On the other hand, if you see a definite and permanent change in attitude or if your child goes through an extended period of making no progress in the sport, you should have a close enough relationship with your child that you can give counsel about the possibility of either changing sports or changing some emphasis.

Some sports, such as gymnastics or swimming, do require a specific body type for success. Children who start those sports when they are quite young may grow into a body type better suited to another sport. One girl started in a private gymnastics club when she was six years old. Since she was a bit larger and stronger than many other girls her age, she was something of a child star. However, as she reached puberty and encountered a rather sudden growth spurt, she gained enough weight and size to make it difficult to perform her gymnastics routines. Through no fault of hers, she wasn't a star anymore. A wise instructor at the club suggested to the girl and her parents that she should explore another activity before she lost her confidence in herself as a person. The girl took his advice and joined a local dance club where she was an immediate success because of the strength and grace she had gained from gymnastics.

This was a wise businessman because he was more interested in the girl than he was in the money she paid for his instruction. If you and your child decide to take advantage of a private sports club, try to find one with this kind of manager. Both of you will be happier.

What Parents Ask

1. *How can I know if my child will enjoy gymnastics enough to be in a private club?*

   Most clubs have an introductory class for that very reason. Call around and see what you can find. This kind of class will let the child experiment before having to make a commitment.

2. *Our daughter has been in a club swim program for four years. Now that she is of high-school age, should she drop out of the private program to get into the school program?*

   That depends on several factors. Ask her and yourself, "Where will she get the best coaching for her ability? Where will she get the challenge and competition she can handle? Where will her friends be?"

3. *There are so many martial arts clubs and schools—judo, karate, taekwando. Which one is the best one for my child?*

   The one he likes! Take your child to visit each kind. Talk to the other students. But don't be pressured. Make sure your athlete has all the information, including what he expects to get out of the program.

21. *The Coach*

"Why blame me? I can't bat and throw for them!" the embittered big league manager cried to the press two days before he was fired. Since there is a human tendency to want to feel sorry for the underdog, most of us probably believed the poor guy. But I am not sure he had an excuse. Losing coaches would have us believe that coaching isn't all that important while winning coaches would have us believe it is everything. Don't you wish those guys would make up their minds?

Although I am not sure how important coaching is in any given situation, I am convinced that a coach has more influence on the performance of players than any other teacher has on the performance of students. Whatever the situation, the coach is in a position to be important.

An old rancher once told me that a good bull is responsible for 5 percent of the quality of the calf crop, but a sorry bull is responsible for 95 percent of the quality of a calf crop. This country formula will probably apply to coaching. A good coach's influence may not be all that conspicuous, but a poor coach's influence is always in evidence.

Since coaching is such an important factor in an athlete's attitude and skill development, you ought to know as much as you can about the people who are and will be coaching your child. Give some attention to them. They will have a lot of influence on your child's attitude toward the game, respect for authority, self-confidence, and skill development. To help you make your evaluation of your child's coach, I have divided the coach's job into three specific roles. Let's begin by taking a look at those roles and how various coaches respond to them.

Coach as a Strategist

Probably the most conspicuous work of a coach is that of a field general. If it is a team sport, the coach draws the Xs and Os and manipulates human bodies as if they were chess pieces. If the sport is an individual one, the coach uses understanding of the sport to engineer all the proper moves and all the training details.

Of course, strategy does make a difference. Games are won and lost on coaching decisions at critical times, and some coaches are better than others at making those important decisions. Unfortunately, however, too often fans, parents, and perhaps even the athletes evaluate a coach's whole ability on this one part of the job while other tasks are just as important, and maybe more so.

Coach as a Teacher

Despite how much natural ability a player may bring to a sport, the player still needs to learn techniques and skills. They need to be learned deeply enough that the athlete will be able to perform in game situations. This is the job of teaching. Some coaches are better at it than others.

Some coaches, the weaker teachers, are constantly surveying their available talent and juggling the players in an attempt to find the right athlete for the right spot. On the other hand, those coaches more comfortable with their teaching skills simply put players in position and teach them how to play those positions.

I once played my teams against a legendary old coach who sent his play book out to all the opposing coaches. He didn't want us to have to go to all the trouble of scouting him through the year. But he didn't make our work easier. He was such a good teacher, and his players were so well trained, that it didn't make any difference that we knew the play he was going to run before he ran it. His team still beat us.

I don't want to deny the role of natural ability here, but frequently a well-trained athlete who uses the right techniques and makes the right decisions in the course of competition will defeat a more naturally gifted athlete who isn't so well trained. This demonstrates the value of good teaching.

Coach as a Motivator

After the coach has developed a game plan with all the Xs and Os drawn in place and has taught the athletes how to carry out their assignments, the next task is getting the athlete or the team mentally ready for the contest. Mental readiness, momentum, intensity—regardless of its name—is a huge determining factor in the outcome of any sports contest, and this makes the coach's task as a motivator very important.

When I was a child, I went to all the sports movies and watched with rapture as the coach made that inspiring locker room speech that moved the team to a miracle; and that scene, repeated in all those movies, inspired me to want to become a coach. Those guys made it look so easy. Just make the plea and those noble young people will run out on the field of honor and win for you. After all these years of coaching, I am still waiting for something like that to happen. Meanwhile, I have discovered that the task of motivation is one of the most mysterious, unpredictable, and controversial aspects of the profession of coaching.

Theories about motivation are as varied as coaches' belt sizes. Some coaches believe they can shame athletes into performance, so they tell the players how worthless and sorry they are. Some coaches believe they can brag athletes into performance, so they use positive verbal reinforcement. Some coaches believe in the noble goal routine so they tell their players about the thousands whose lives and happiness depend on a win. Some coaches believe that game preparation is something of a sacred ritual, so they insist on a quiet, reflective time. Some coaches believe in mob frenzy, so they use chants or cries or bizarre irrational acts. Some coaches believe in gimmicks or tokens such as "splatches" on a helmet for a good performance.

When your child is playing for a particular coach, you must know how that coach approaches the role of motivator. What is said and done to try to get the athletes to perform to their potential? This characteristic, more than teaching ability or ability with the Xs and Os, will affect a coach's behavior and image and ultimately his or her position as a positive influence and teacher for your child. If your child's coach is doing a good job in the other two areas of coaching but is failing or overreacting in this area, you will need to be in a position to explain his actions to your young athlete and help that athlete work through any barriers.

By this time, you probably want to ask, "But why does the coach have so much influence over the athlete? Why is that relationship so important? Isn't the coach just another teacher?"

Usually, for most athletes at least, the coach-player relationship is different from any other adult-child relationship simply because of the role sports plays in the child's life. As I have said, competition will eventually bring out the true character in the athlete. Somewhere in the course of the practice or game, the athlete will lower the facades, expose weaknesses, and make a commitment to the best effort possible. Victory and defeat, both rare moments in the process of growth will be experienced in the presence of the coach. In the midst of all this honesty, openness, vulnerability, and commitment, the athlete becomes almost completely dependent upon the coach, emotionally, intellectually, and physically.

By the nature of the sport itself, the coach plays a powerful role in the life of any athlete who makes a commitment to the sport. The coach who is not sensitive to the total meaning of that power is not fit to coach. Unfortunately, some aren't. I hope your child never gets one, but if that does happen, you can still salvage the joys and lessons of sports by becoming the most ardent, helpful fan any athlete ever had.

How am I doing as a motivator so far? Have I scared you into wanting to know how you can get a closer look at this person who is going to have what could be a powerful and lasting influence on your child's growth? Good. Actually, there is a rather simple formula for examining a coach's influence because the distinctives that separate one coach from another can be reduced to two simple categories: integrity and relationship.

We coaches would like to think there is more—that we are the world's greatest geniuses at drawing Xs and Os and that our players should be eternally grateful for the privilege of playing under our brilliance; or that we are the world's greatest teachers of skills and techniques. But to the players, one coach is different from another only in the areas of integrity or relationship.

Every year a player comes to me at the end of the season, and I can tell by the look in his eye that he has a compliment for me. That's nice. At my age those compliments are about as vital to my health as a daily glass of orange juice. They help keep me going. But I always try to prepare myself for what I am going to hear.

I always think this player is going to say something about my knowledge of teaching blocking skills or my skill at organizing a practice or my ability to outfox the opponent in the middle of a game. But I never hear those things. Instead, the player says something like, "Thank you for talking to me about why I didn't make the first team. Thank you for being approachable. Thank you for letting us laugh during practice. Thank you for not using profanity."

Do you see my point? What stands out in the athlete's mind and makes me different from other coaches he has had throughout his life is in the area of integrity or relationship. Since those are the areas where your child will evaluate a coach, let's talk about each one individually.

Integrity

Don't be deceived. If your child is about to enter a potentially powerful relationship with another human being, you don't need to worry about the won-lost record, the on-field strategy, or even the person's private charm. The first thing you will want to know is whether this is a person of integrity. You are trusting this person with your most precious possession, your athlete who will live after you and stand as a living testimony of the kind of person you are.

Does this coach have personal integrity? How does this coach look at himself and his own commitments? What kind of discipline does he have? Is he a person of his word? Is he willing to make a sacrifice for what he believes in? Be assured. Somewhere in the course of their career together, that coach is going to ask your child to make a sacrifice. Is the coach worth it? Has he earned the right to make the demand?

Frankly, I have never been impressed by coaches who stand in dressing rooms yelling at their players for lacking courage and character. Something doesn't match up. There is a lack of personal integrity. Regardless of whether your young athlete knows it, this is making a definite mental imprint. The relationship between the coach and athlete is too close, too honest, for such a thing as this to go by unnoticed.

One of my students stopped by for a chat. I could tell that she was rather depressed. Eventually, she told me her story. When she was in high school, she had developed a special relationship with a particular teacher. This teacher had been sensitive to some of the student's fears and needs and had engineered a rather open and honest relationship between the two. He had taught the girl how to find confidence and courage; and with his encouragement through believing in her, she went on to distinguish herself as a college student.

But then she heard that this teacher was getting a divorce. Her fortress of sensitivity, understanding, and courage crumbled. She was devastated by the news. You may protest that she was overreacting. She didn't know the circumstances. That may be true, but through that honest relationship, like the one the coach will have with your child, that teacher had built himself an image of indestructibility. When he showed his human frailty, he betrayed his image in that student's mind.

Does this coach have integrity toward the sport itself? This is usually easy to see and judge. Some coaches approach their job with full respect toward the spirit of the sport. They like the game and what it stands for. They are more interested in playing the game as it is supposed to be played than in ultimate outcome. They don't take advantage of the rules. They don't design trick plays that border on being illegal. They don't teach players how to cheat without getting caught. They don't yell at officials when the officials are right. They don't trap their players between the player's own sense of integrity and the coach's approach to the sport.

A few years ago, a high-school student came to me for advice. This student's writing teacher wanted one of his students to be published in a statewide magazine. So the teacher wrote his own poem and sent it to the judges under the name of the student. Of course, the student was selected for an honor and a position he didn't deserve. He didn't know how to handle the dilemma. Obviously, that teacher had no respect for the student or for the spirit of the publication. Would you trust your child to a coach who would do something like that?

Relationships

To the athletes one of the most important and distinctive characteristics of a coach is the style of relationships with athletes. Since this area is so important to your child, you will want to understand just what approach the coach uses. Of course, you can't just ask the coach. But you can discover this style by observing the coach during practice and contests and by listening to your child talk around the dinner table and with fellow players in the car pool. If you tune in, you can usually get a feel for the kind of relationship the coach has with the team as a whole. Then, you will not only understand, but you may also be in a position to lend some support as your child struggles through trying to understand the character of the relationship.

This, too, is easier than you may think. Coaching relationships fall somewhere into three general categories: the control relationship, the cooperative relationship, and the confused relationship.

1. The control relationship. Some coaches are in charge. They control the way players dress, eat, move, run, shoot, play, pick their teeth, or scratch while on national television. They approach the coach-player relationship with rules, authority, and enough distance to make the authority work. In a control relationship, there is no doubt in the player's mind that the coach is in charge. The player also knows that the coach can be pleased by doing exactly what the coach says.

Most of the players who have such coaches respect them because they know exactly where they stand, both in the sport and with the coach. Often the control relationship coach is successful in winning games, too.

2. The cooperative relationship. The other side of the control relationship is the cooperative relationship. These coaches usually communicate to their athletes that the sport is a joint venture. They appeal to virtues other than mere obedience to motivate athletes to learn and perform. They develop a relationship that will permit the players to express their opinions about practice or game strategy. They spend a lot of their time working one on one with players and recognizing each player's individual talents, mood, and backgrounds.

Most of these coaches are respected and liked by their players. They, too, are often quite successful in winning contests.

3. The confused relationship. Somewhere between the control relationship and the cooperative relationship is that poor coach who either hasn't thought about or can't decide what kind of relationship he or she wants to have. The result is a confused coach with a horde of confused athletes. One moment the coach asks for opinions and the next moment yells directions and asserts needless authority.

Any athlete in a confused relationship will have to work at finding happiness in the sport. Since the athlete has to invest so much in the sport, emotional health depends on having some kind of understanding of where he or she fits. When the coach isn't sure, the player will always be plagued with anxieties. The coach may protest that those anxieties make the athlete hungry and eager. But an anxious child isn't much fun around the house on a Saturday morning. If your child is playing for a coach who always keeps the athletes on edge, you will want to be particularly sensitive to the child's need for reassurance. Take the job yourself. Pat your child on the back once in awhile.

Now that you have all this information about how to analyze a coach, remember to treat him like a human being. Some of them actually are, and those who aren't are close enough to respond to the compliment. When the coach is right and good, write a note or make a phone call. When he is rotten, do the same. But when you point out flaws, you are now in a better position to make specific suggestions.

In the meantime, make sure you realize the potential power that coach has over your child, and constantly observe and monitor that child's growth and happiness in the sport. That is what the office of parent of an athlete is all about.

What Parents Ask

1. *My daughter's high-school coach is not a very good motivator. What do I do?*

   You probably have to live with that deficiency. What you always do is look at the strengths and weaknesses any given coach has. No coach is perfect. In this case, make sure you and your daughter accent the positive about the coach, and you do what you can to motivate your daughter yourself.

2. *I would like to thank the coach for what he is doing for our son, but won't this look like I am just playing up to him?*

   No. Sincere compliments are never in bad taste. Coaches, to be effective, need to believe in themselves. Coaches need to be reminded that their focus is right. Coaches need to know someone notices. Don't ever be afraid to commend a coach, in season or out.

3. *Are coaches ever lonely?*

   All the time! Coaching is a lonely profession. Every day, a coach has to make thousands of decisions—about strategy, teaching, or motivation. Since he has to live with those decisions, he has to have the freedom to make those decisions himself. Thus, he has to do most of his thinking in a closet somewhere.

22. *The Final Transition*

For the really successful athlete, for the one who gets the most out of the sport and is most fervently involved, the most difficult moment in the sport, and maybe in life, is that single inevitable moment when it comes time to quit. We have all witnessed this tragic scene so many times that we can support it with thousands of illustrations. The once-great professional has lost ability, speed, judgment, grace, and the right to stardom, but he hangs on, trying to play one more season, trying to be good enough just to stay in the sport now that he can no longer be a star.

Of course, only the great ones get the publicity and the public sympathy, but the same story goes on thousands of times every year in dressing rooms throughout the world. It comes time to quit, hang it up, check it in. For the athlete who has chosen to spend all that time in a sport that does have to end, the transition is rarely an easy one.

Throughout this book, I have talked about the emotional thrills, the social distinctions, and the positive self-identity to be achieved through participation in a sport. When it comes time to shut oneself off from that supply of psychological help, one could go into a state of depression.

If you want to help your child all through life and not only through childhood and adolescence, you need to think about that moment when your child will reach quitting time. You as a parent will especially need to anticipate that time, because no one else will. As your child is tearing up the basketball court at sixteen and devastating all opponents, he or she simply can't imagine a time when basketball and its psychological rewards will not be there. You will have to see into the future for your child.

Don't underestimate the role sports can play in the athlete's life. Of-

179

ten an athlete can become addicted to the highs of playing and will suffer withdrawal symptoms when it comes time to quit. Let's ponder why this happens.

Some people thrive on the competition, the going head to head, the risk taking, the winning or losing. These people not only get their acknowledgment and positive feedback from competition, but they also use it as their source of motivation. Most of what they are is related to that competition and how they handle it.

Sports are an acceptable outlet for that compelling competitive spirit. But when the opportunity to play ends or is drastically altered by age and circumstances, people who have been so dependent on competition will have to work at adjusting.

Many athletes have been in sports for a long time or since they were very young. Some of them achieve all their glory, all their distinction from sports. They simply don't know how to achieve a feeling of self-worth or distinction without the sports performance.

Some people use sports participation to break up the routine of day-to-day living. After so many months and so many years, workdays and even marriage days can begin to look alike. The joy of living, if there is to be any joy, must be carved out of and into that routine.

On the other hand, sports are rarely routine, for the athlete at least. Every game is a highlight, an unusual event, a distinctive moment. So long as the athlete has sports, those memorable moments will be there to serve as stepping stones across the puddles of routine living. But what does life have to offer when those opportunities are gone?

Let me offer you some suggestions to help your child prepare for that time when active sports participation will come to an end.

Have Other Sports Interests

Make sure your child develops sports interests outside of those competitive sports that have a definite ending. Sports such as football and basketball will end when middle age sets in or athletes graduate from school programs or grow too old for the park district. But other sports such as tennis, running, or golf don't ever have to end. I call these lifetime sports, and the list of what is available is longer than you or your young athlete might expect.

One of the top female athletes in our college stopped by my office for a chat. When she came to college, she was a three-sport athlete, something of a star in volleyball, basketball, and track. As a sophomore, she gave up volleyball and basketball to concentrate on making herself one of the finest hurdlers in the nation, and she has achieved her goal.

In the course of our conversation, she said something very wise. "Sometime this spring, I will run the last hurdle race of my life. I know that. And that will create a big hole in my being. But I have already begun to explore the merits of long distance road racing, so I won't have to lose that part of my life that running hurdles has filled."

Now that is a smart lady. I would guess that she has understanding parents or coaches who have helped her see the final race before she gets to it.

Develop a Positive Self-Image

While you are helping your child find enjoyment in a variety of sports, some of which are lifetime sports, you can also help your child develop a positive self-image apart from sports. Make sure your child participates in rewarding activities. Again, let's look at that illustration of the old pros. Notice how some can retire gracefully while others can't. If you read the biography carefully, you will usually find that the difference is in the fact that some athletes have built a life for themselves outside of sports and some haven't. Never let your child grow that one-dimensional.

Get into the Coaching Profession

Counsel your child into a coaching profession. Then, when age declares that it's time to move on, your athlete can always write a book about the experiences of a lifetime. We jest, but only partly.

After a collective total of more than eighty years as players, coaches, and parents of athletes, we, the authors of this book, still look at sports as a delightful pastime for all children everywhere, regardless of age. We have attempted to convey to you that being an athlete, dedicated or casual, talented or struggling, can be one of the most significant experiences in any person's life. We hope your child can find all the joys, fun, lessons, and rewards that sports participation has to offer. We hope you find the joys of being a parent of an athlete. And may none of us—coaches, fans, and parents—ever forget that whatever happens, that athlete is still "some mother's baby."

What Parents Ask

1. *What do coaches do when they get too old to coach?*

   The good-looking ones become television commentators. The others write books about sports.